Polish
PHRASE
BOOK

Hania Forss

Consultant:

Jonathan Fowler

BBC B

Contents

How to use this book   5

The Polish alphabet   7

Pronunciation   8

General conversation   12

Arriving in the country   17

Changing money   19

Directions   21

Road travel   24

  Car and bicycle parts   30

Taxis   33

Buses and coaches   35

Travelling by train   38

Air travel   43

Boats and ferries   46

At the tourist office   49

Accommodation   51

Telephones   58

Eating and drinking   61

Menu reader   67

Business trips   73

Shopping   76

Sightseeing   83

Sports and activities   86

Health 90
Parts of the body 94
Problems and complaints 97
Basic grammar 103
Numbers 114
Days, months, dates 118
Time 122
Countries and nationalities 124
General signs and notices 127
Conversion tables 129
National holidays 133
Useful addresses 134
English-Polish Dictionary 136
Emergencies 188
All-purpose phrases 190

How to use this book

▌ Communicating in a foreign language doesn't have to be difficult – you can convey a lot with just a few words (plus a few gestures and a bit of mime). Just remember: keep it simple. Don't try to come out with long, grammatically perfect sentences when one or two words will get your meaning across.

▌ On pages 190–191 is a list of All-purpose phrases. Some will help you to make contact, for example with greetings, 'please' and 'thank you', 'yes' and 'no'. Some are to get people to help you understand what they're saying to you. And some are questions like 'Do you have ...?', to which you can add words from the Dictionary at the back of the book.

▌ The book is divided into sections for different situations, such as Road travel, Shopping, Health and so on. In each section you'll find:

Useful tips and information

Words and phrases that you'll see on signs or in print

Phrases you are likely to want to say

Things that people may say to you

▌ Many of the phrases can be adapted by simply using another word from the Dictionary. For instance, take the question **Czy daleko do lotniska?** (Is it far to the airport?: **czy** is a question word, **daleko** means 'far' and **do lotniska** means 'to the airport'). If you want to know if the *station* is far away, just substitute **stacji** (the station) for **lotniska** to give **Czy daleko do stacji?**

▌ All the phrases have a simple pronunciation guide alongside them based on English sounds – this is explained in Pronunciation (page 8).

▌ If you want some guidance on how the Polish language works, see Basic grammar, page 103

■ You'll notice that sometimes two forms of verbs are used in the phrases: this is because Polish has slightly different verb endings (in the past tense), depending on whether the speaker is male or female, and whether it's a woman or a man being spoken to or referred to. Also remember that Polish uses a formal way of address if you don't know someone well: you use the form **pan** when directly addressing a man and **pani** when addressing a woman.

■ There is a handy reference section (starting on page 114) which contains lists of days and months, countries and nationalities, general signs and notices that you'll see, conversion tables, national holidays, numbers and useful addresses.

■ There is an English-Polish dictionary starting on page 136.

■ There is an Emergencies section (which we hope you *won't* have to use) on pages 188–189.

■ Wherever possible, work out in advance what you want to say – if you're going shopping, for instance, write out a shopping list in Polish. If you're buying travel tickets, work out how to say where you want to go, how many tickets you want, single or return, etc.

■ Practise saying things out loud – the cassette that goes with this book will help you to get used to the sound of Polish.

■ Above all – don't be shy! It'll be appreciated if you try to say a few words, even if it's only 'good morning' and 'goodbye' – and in fact those are the very sorts of phrases that are worth learning, as you'll hear them and need to use them all the time.

■ The authors would welcome any suggestions or comments about this book, but in the meantime, have a good trip – **przyjemnych wakacji!**

The Polish alphabet

▌ Polish has some letters marked with additonal signs over, or under them, to indicate different pronunciation: **ą, ę, ć, ł, ń, ó, ś, ź,** and **ż.** The letters **q, v, x** don't exist in Polish and are found only in some words of foreign origin.

Letter	Pronounced	Letter	Pronounced
A	a	O	o
Ą	aw	Ó	oo
B	be	P	pe
C	tse	R	er
Ć	che	S	es
D	de	Ś	esh
E	e	T	te
Ę	eng	U	oo
F	ef	W	voo
G	ge	Y	i
H	ha	Z	zet
I	ee	Ź	zhet
J	yot	Ż	zhet
K	ka		
L	el		
Ł	ew		
M	em		
N	en		
Ń	enh		

Pronunciation

❚ You don't need perfect pronunciation to be able to communicate – it's enough to get the sounds approximately right and use the correct word stress. If you want to hear real Polish voices and practise the pronunciation, you can listen to the cassette.

❚ Polish pronunciation and spelling is more consistent than English and, in most cases, each letter corresponds to one sound. What makes Polish sound and, when written, look difficult at the first encounter are: certain groups of consonants occurring together in combinations unusual for an English person, e.g. **psz**, **szcz**, **chc**, and some letters marked with additional signs over or under them to indicate different pronunciation e.g. **ś**, **ć**, **ą**, **ę**.

Stress

In the majority of words stress falls on the second syllable from the end: **Warszawa**, **samolot**. Words of foreign origin tend to have their stress on the 3rd syllable from the end: *muzyka*, *uniwersytet*. Stressed syllables are marked throughout this book.

Vowels

There are two vowels with exactly the same pronunciation, u and ó, and two nasal vowels, ą and ę. The pronunciation of the nasal vowels varies, depending on the sounds immediately following them, and on their position in the word. **ę** in the middle of a word is pronounced *en* , e.g. **ręka** (hand) – *renka*; at the end of a word it is pronounced *eh*: **proszę** (please) – *prosheh*. **ą** in the middle of a word is pronounced *on* or *om*: **książka** – *kshonshka*, **kąpiel** – *kompyel*; at the end of the word it is pronounced *o*: **są** (are) – *so*.

8

	Approx. English equivalent	Shown in book as	Example	Pronounced as
a	a in 'cat'	a	tak	*tak*
ą (nasal)	on in 'bond',	on	mąka,	*monka,*
	om in 'Tom',	om	kąpiel	*kompyel*
	o in 'so'	o	są	*so*
e	e in 'met'	e	cena	*tsena*
ę (nasal)	en in 'Bengali',	en	ręka,	*renka,*
	e in 'met'	eh	proszę	*prosheh*
i	ee in 'meet'	ee	bilet	*beelet*
o	o in 'lot'	o	motor	*motor*
ó ⎫ u ⎭	oo in 'booth'	oo oo	Bóg buty	*book* *booti*
y	i in 'lip'	i	rynek	*rinek*

Consonants

Most consonants are pronounced in a similar way to English. However, since some of them have signs over them, or occur in certain combinations which affect their pronunciation, they are presented in this book in four different groups, according to their pronunciation pattern. Remember that all voiced consonants, such as **b**, **d**, **g**, **z**, **w**, **ż** and **rz**, are pronounced as voiceless: *p, t, k, s, f* and *sh* at the end of a word or in the middle, depending on the neighbouring sounds, e.g. **klub** – *kloop*, **kwiat** – *kfyat*, **lekarz** – *lekash*. The consonants **h** and **ch** have the same pronunciation: as *h* in 'high'. Similarly, **rz** and **ż** are pronounced in the same way: as final *g* in 'garage', or *sh* as in 'shut'. The Polish **r** is always hard and rolled, rather like Scottish.

1. The following consonants are pronounced almost as in English:

	Approx. English equivalent	Shown in book as	Example	Pronounced as
b	b in 'but'	b	bank	*bank*
	or p in 'cup'	p	klub	*kloop*
d	d in 'day'	d	dobry	*dobri*
	or t in 'ten'	t	kod	*kot*
f	f in 'fit'	f	filtr	*feeltr*
g	g in 'gas'	g	gaz	*gas*
	or k in 'kit'	k	Bóg	*book*
h	h in 'high'	h	herbata	*herbata*
k	k in 'kit'	k	kot	*kot*
l	l in 'luck'	l	lewo	*levo*
m	m in 'met'	m	matka	*matka*
n	n in 'no'	n	narty	*narti*
p	p in 'put'	p	praca	*pratsa*
s	s in 'stick'	s	sto	*sto*
t	t in 'tin'	t	tam	*tam*
z	z in 'zone'	z	zoo	*zoo*
	or s in 'set'	s	wóz	*voos*

2. The following Polish consonants are pronounced differently in English:

c	ts in 'fits'	ts	cena	*tsena*
ch	h in 'high'	h	Chiny	*heeni*
j	y in 'yes'	y	jeść	*yeshch*
ł	w in 'wit'	w	ławka	*wafka*
r	r in 'pray'	r	praca	*pratsa*
w	v in 'vine'	v	wino	*veeno*
	or f in 'lift'	f	krew	*kref*
ż	s in 'measure'	zh	żona	*zhona*
	or sh in 'fish'	sh	też	*tesh*

3. The next group of consonants is distinguished by an accent over them, which indicates a soft pronunciation, much softer than in English:

ć	ch in 'cheek'	ch	nić	*neech*
ń	n in 'onion'	n	koń	*kon*
ś	s in 'sugar'	sh	ktoś	*ktosh*
ź	final g in 'garage'	zh	źle	*zhle*

4. The consonants below are represented by two letters, and are much harder than in English (except the last **dź**, which is soft):

cz	ch in 'check'	ch	czek	*chek*
sz	sh in 'shop'	sh	szukać	*shookach*
rz	final g in 'garage'	zh	rzeka	*zheka*
dz	ds in 'needs'	dz	dzbanek	*dzbanek*
dż	j in 'jam'	dj	dżem	*djem*
dź	j in 'jeans'	dj	dźwig	*djveek*

There are also some typical consonant groups in Polish which do not exist in English in the same combinations. They represent two, sometimes three, sounds and are very common:

chrz	h in 'high' + sh in 'shop'	hsh	chrząstka	*hshonstka*
krz	k in 'kit' + sh in 'shop'	ksh	krzyk	*kshik*
szcz	sh in 'shop' + ch in 'check'	shch	szczyt	*shchit*
trz	t in 'tin' + s h in 'shop'	tsh	trzy	*tshi*

Note

For the sake of simplicity, the sounds ż and ź are shown as *zh*; ć and cz as *ch*; ń as *n*; dź and dż as *dj*.

❚ To greet someone, you use the phrase **dzień dobry** (good day) from early morning till early evening, after which you say **dobry wieczór** (good evening).You can use these phrases for both formal and informal occasions.

❚ A common informal phrase, used among friends for both greetings and leave-taking, is **cześć** ('hello,' or 'bye'), pronounced *cheshch*.

❚ When leave-taking, you say **do widzenia** (goodbye), **do zobaczenia** (see you), or **dobranoc** (good night), when it is late.

❚ When it comes to addressing a person directly, you use the formal **pan** (Mr) or **pani** (Mrs or Miss) forms, when you are speaking to adults whom you haven't met before or know only slightly, e.g. **gdzie pan** (male)/**pani** (female) **pracuje?** (where do you work?) In this book, many phrases have the **pan/pani** forms, since it is assumed you don't know the people you meet in Poland.

❚ However, as in other European languages, there is a tendency among young people not to use these formal forms. In this case, you might address a young person using the informal **ty** ('you' singular), or **wy** ('you' plural), e.g. **gdzie ty pracujesz?** ('where do you live?' singular) and **gdzie wy pracujecie?** ('where do you live?' plural). Similarly, you might yourself be addressed in this informal way. **Ty** and **wy** can be omitted in a sentence.

❚ If you want to attract someone's attention in the street, you can say **proszę pana/pani**, or simply **przepraszam** (excuse me).

❚ Polish has different forms to indicate sex distinctions, e.g. **Anglik** (Englishman), **Angielka** (English woman), **student** (male student), **studentka** (female student). In this book, both forms are given, the masculine form first, then the feminine. Furthermore, the verbal forms also express the sex distinctions as different verb endings in the past tense, depending on whether the speaker is a man or a woman, e.g. a man will say: **przyjechałem wczoraj** (I arrived yesterday), whereas a woman will say: **przyjechałam wczoraj**.

Greetings and leave taking; attracting attention

Welcome	Witam	*veetam*
Welcome (informal)	Cześć	*cheshch*
Good morning	Dzień dobry	*djen dobry*
Good evening	Dobry wieczór	*dobri vyechoor*
How are you?	Co słychać?	*tso swihach*
Fine, thanks	Dobrze, dziękuję	*dobzhe djenkooyeh*
And you?	A pan (male)/pani (female)?	*a pan/panee*
Goodbye	Do widzenia	*do veedzenya*
See you	Do zobaczenia	*do zobachenya*
Good night	Dobranoc	*dobranots*
Excuse me!	Proszę pana (male)/pani (female) or przepraszam!	*prosheh pana/panee; psheprasham*

Introductions

My name is ...	Nazywam się ...	*nazivam sheh*
Nice to meet you	Miło mi poznać	*meewo mee poznach*
This is my wife/daughter	To moja żona/córka	*to moya zhona/tsoorka*
This is my husband/son	To mój mąż/syn	*to mooy monsh/sin*
These are my children	To moje dzieci	*to moye djechee*

Talking about yourself and your family

(see Countries and nationalities, page 124)

I am English	Jestem Anglikiem (male)/Angielką (female)	*yestem angleekyem/angyelko*
I live in London	Mieszkam w Londynie	*myeshkam v londinye*
I'm a student	Jestem studentem (male)/studentką (female)	*yestem stoodentem/stoodentko*
I'm a tourist	Jestem turystą	*yestem tooristo*
I work in ...	Pracuję w ...	*pratsooyeh v*

13

I work in an office	**Pracuję w biurze**	*pratsooyeh v byoozhe*
I'm on holiday	**Jestem na wakacjach/** (student) or **jestem na urlopie** (if working)	*yestem na vakatsyah /yestem na oorlopye*
I'm here on business	**Jestem tu służbowo**	*yestem too swoozhbovo*
I arrived yesterday	**Przyjechałem** (male) **wczoraj** or **Przyjechałam** (female) **wczoraj**	*pshiyehawem fchoray/ pshiyehawam fchoray*
I don't speak much Polish	**Mówię mało po polsku**	*moovyeh mawo po polskoo*

You may hear

Jak się pan (male)/**pani** (female)**nazywa?**	*yak sheh pan/panee naziva*	What's your name?
Skąd pan/pani jest?	*skont pan/panee yest*	Where are you from?
Jak długo w Polsce?	*yak dwoogo f polstse*	How long are you staying in Poland?
Jak się podoba Polska?	*yak sheh podoba polska*	How do you like Poland?

Talking about Poland and your own country

Poland is very beautiful	**Polska jest bardzo piękna**	*polska yest bardzo pyenkna*
I know Poland well	**Znam Polskę dobrze**	*znam polskeh dobzhe*
It's my first visit	**Jestem tu po raz pierwszy**	*yestem too po ras pyerfshi*
Are you from here?	**Czy pan** (male)/**pani** (female) **jest stąd?**	*chi pan/panee yest stont*
Have you been to England?	**Czy był pan**(male)/**była pani** (female) **w Anglii?**	*chi biw pan/biwa panee v anglee*
Did you like England?	**Podobała się Anglia?**	*podobawa sheh anglya*

You may hear

Pierwszy raz w Polsce?	*pyerfshi ras f polstse*	Is this your first visit to Poland?
Gdzie pan (male)/**pani** (female) **pracuje?**	*gdje pan/panee pratsooye*	Where do you work?

Likes and dislikes

Note: there are two expressions for 'to like' – **lubić**, which carries a slightly emotional attitude, and **podobać się**, which is more neutral in tone.

I like swimming	**Lubię pływać**	*loobyeh pwivach*
I don't like cold weather	**Nie lubię zimnej pogody**	*nye loobyeh zheemney pogodi*
I like this dress	**Ta suknia podoba mi się**	*ta sooknya podoba mee sheh*

Talking to a child

What's your name?	**Jak się nazywasz?**	*yak sheh nazivash*
How old are you?	**Ile masz lat?**	*eele mash lat*
Do you have any brothers or sisters?	**Czy masz braci i siostry?**	*chi mash brachee ee shostri*

Invitations and replies

Would you like a drink?	**Podać coś do picia?**	*podach tsosh do peecha*
Yes, please	**Tak, proszę**	*tak prosheh*
No, thank you	**Nie, dziękuję**	*nye djenkooyeh*
I'd love to	**Bardzo chętnie**	*bardzo hentnye*
That's very kind of you	**To miło z pana** (male)/**pani** (female) **strony**	*to meewo s pana /panee stroni*
Please leave me alone	**Proszę dać mi spokój**	*prosheh dach mee spokooy*

You may hear

Podać coś do picia?	*podach tsosh do peecha*	Would you like a drink?
Podać coś do jedzenia?	*podach tsosh do yedzenya*	Would you like something to eat?

Good wishes and exclamations

Congratulations!	**Gratulacje!**	*gratoolatsye*
Best wishes!	**Najlepsze życzenia!**	*naylepshe zhichenya*
It's wonderful!	**Cudownie!**	*tsoodovnye*
Happy Christmas!	**Szczęśliwych Świąt!**	*shchenshleevih shfyont*
Good luck!	**Powodzenia!**	*povodzenya*
Have a good journey!	**Szczęśliwej podróży!**	*shchenshleevey podroozhi*
Enjoy your meal!	**Smacznego!**	*smachnego*
Cheers! (your health)	**Na zdrowie**	*na zdrovye*
What a pity!	**Szkoda**	*shkoda*

Talking about the weather

What a lovely day!	**Ale piękny dzień**	*ale pyenkni djen*
What terrible weather!	**Ale okropna pogoda**	*ale okropna pogoda*
It's going to rain	**Będzie padać**	*bendje padach*
It's hot, isn't it?	**Gorąco, prawda?**	*gorontso, pravda*
It's cold, isn't it?	**Zimno, prawda?**	*zheemno, pravda*

■ Passport control and customs are straightforward. You need a full British passport, issued by the Home Office; a British Visitor's Passport is not valid in Poland. Holders of full British passports do not need visas. People entering Poland are obliged, however, to register in their place of stay within 48 hours of crossing the border. Registration is performed by the hotel, or campsite reception desk, or by whoever is responsible for your accommodation. Otherwise, proper registration authorities should be notified, e.g. the nearest police station.

■ You will probably not need to say anything in Polish unless you are asked the purpose of your visit or have something to declare at the customs. If you need to say what you have to declare, look up the words you need in the Dictionary. You can get a leaflet at your point of departure giving details of duty-free items.

You may see

Dworzec Autobusowy	Bus station
Dworzec Kolejowy	Railway station
Informacja turystyczna	Tourist information
Kontrola celna	Customs control
Kontrola paszportowa	Passport control
Nic do oclenia	Nothing to declare
Palenie wzbronione or **Prosimy nie palić**	No smoking
Taksówki	Taxis
Towary do oclenia	Goods to declare

You may want to say

I'm here on holiday	**Jestem tu na urlopie**	*yestem too na oorlopye*
I'm here on business	**Jestem służbowo**	*yestem swoozhbovo*
I've got something to declare	**Mam coś do oclenia**	*mam tsosh do otslenya*
I haven't got anything to declare	**Nie mam nic do oclenia**	*nye mam neets do otslenya*
I have two bottles of whisky	**Mam dwie butelki whisky**	*mam dvye bootelkee weeskee*
I have a receipt	**Mam rachunek**	*mam rahoonek*

You may hear

Paszport, proszę	*pashport prosheh*	Passport, please
Dokumenty, proszę	*dokoomenti prosheh*	Documents, please
Jaki cel wizyty?	*jakee tsel veeziti*	Purpose of visit?
Na jak długo do Polski?	*na yak dwoogo do polskee*	How long are you staying in Poland?

Changing money

▌ The Polish currency is the **złoty**, abbreviated most commonly to '**zł**', or sometimes (e.g. when you write on Eurocheques) '**PZL**'.

▌ Money can be changed at a **Kantor** (a place where you change currency), which can be found in some banks, hotels and shops, as well as in separate premises. The rates of exchange are normally listed by the entrance or in the window: '**skup**' shows the rate at which currency is bought and '**sprzedaż**' the rate at which it is sold. Kantors take cash in note form only, and don't usually charge a commission. The opening hours vary: generally 9.00 a.m. to 6.00 p.m. on weekdays, and 9.00 a.m. to 2.00 p.m. on Saturdays.

▌ Banks are open from 8 a.m. to 7 p.m. Mondays to Fridays, and from 9 a.m. to 1 p.m. on Saturdays. It is only possible to cash Eurocheques or make credit card withdrawals over the counter in certain banks. You have to show your passport.

▌ Traveller's cheques can be changed in the larger hotels or at an American Express office.

▌ With regard to the availability of Eurocheque etc. facilities outside Warsaw, it's best to phone the relevant bank in your own country to get the most recent information.

▌ Cash dispensers are not yet widespread in Poland.

You may see

Kantor	A money exchange bureau
Kasa	Cashier
Otwarty	Open
Skup	The rate at which currency is bought
Sprzedaż	The rate at which currency is sold
Wymiana pieniędzy/waluty	Bureau de change

You may want to say

(See also Numbers, page...)

I'd like to change some pounds sterling	**Chcę wymienić funty angielskie**	*htseh vimyeneech foonti angyelskye*
I'd like to change some traveller's cheques	**Chcę wymienić czeki podróżne**	*htseh vimyeneech chekee podroozhne*
I'd like to cash a Eurocheque	**Chcę wymienić Euroczek**	*htseh vimyeneech yoorochek*
I'd like to get some cash	**Chcę podjąć pieniądze na kartę kredytową**	*htseh podyonch pyenyondze na karteh kreditovo*
What's the exchange rate today?	**Jaki dzisiaj kurs wymiany?**	*yakee djeeshay koors vimyani*
Can you give me some change, please?	**Czy mogę dostać drobne?**	*chi mogeh dostach drobne*
I'm staying at the Sokrates Hotel	**Mieszkam w hotelu Sokrates**	*myeshkam f hoteloo sokrates*
I'm staying with friends	**Mieszkam u znajomych**	*myeshkam oo znayomih*
The address is Plac Konstytucji, 125	**Mój adres jest Plac Konstytucji, sto dwadzieścia pięć**	*mooy adres yest plats konstitootsyee sto dvadjeshcha pyench*

You may hear

Ile chce pan/pani wymienić?	*eele htseh pan/panee vimyeneech*	How much do you want to change?
Proszę paszport	*prosheh pashport*	Your passport, please
Proszę iść do kasy	*prosheh eeshch do kasi*	Please go to the cashier
Proszę tu podpisać	*prosheh too potpeesach*	Sign here, please

Directions

▮ Most towns have tourist information offices, where you can buy general or specialized maps and guides. These can also be purchased at bookshops.

▮ When you want to ask for directions, the best way to attract attention is by saying: **przepraszam** (excuse me), followed by: **gdzie jest ...?** (where is ...?), e.g. **Przepraszam, gdzie jest bank?** (Excuse me, where is the bank?).

▮ In trying to understand the answer, listen out for the most important bits of information, e.g. far, not far, right, left, etc. If you can't understand anything, ask the person to repeat the directions, by saying: **Proszę powtórzyć**.

▮ If you are looking for a particular address, have it written down. In Poland, addresses are written with the name of the street first, followed by the number of the block or house, followed by the flat number, e.g. **ul. Marszałkowska 179 m. 42.**

You may see

Aleja	Avenue
Katedra	Cathedral
Kościół	Church
Muzeum	Museum
Pałac	Palace
Plac	Square
Przejście dla pieszych	Pedestrian crossing
Ratusz	Town Hall
Ulica (ul.)	Street
Zamek	Castle

You may want to say

Excuse me	**Przepraszam**	*psheprasham*
Pardon?	**Słucham?**	*swooham*
Could you repeat that, please?	**Proszę powtórzyć**	*prosheh poftoozhich*
Slowly	**Wolno**	*volno*
Again	**Jeszcze raz**	*yeshche ras*
I'm lost	**Zgubiłem się** (male)/ **Zgubiłam się** (female)	*zgoobeewem sheh/ zgoobeewam sheh*
Where is ...?	**Gdzie jest ...?**	*gdje yest*
Where are ...?	**Gdzie są ...?**	*gdje so*
Where are we?	**Gdzie jesteśmy?**	*gdje yesteshmi*
Where is it?	**Gdzie to jest?**	*gdje to yest*
Where is the bank?	**Gdzie jest bank?**	*gdje yest bank*
Where are the taxis?	**Gdzie są taksówki?**	*gdje so taxoofkee*
Where are the toilets?	**Gdzie są ubikacje?**	*gdje so oobeekatsye*
Is there a ... near here?	**Czy jest tu blisko ...?**	*chi yest too bleesko*
Please show me on the map	**Proszę pokazać na mapie**	*prosheh pokazach na mapye*
How do you get to the airport?	**Jak dojechać na lotnisko?**	*yak doyehach na lotneesko*
How do you get to the station?	**Jak dojść do dworca?**	*yak doyshch do dvortsa*
Is this the road to Kraków?	**Czy to droga do Krakowa?**	*chi to droga do krakova*
Is it far?	**Czy to daleko?**	*chi to daleko*
Is it near?	**Czy to blisko?**	*chi to bleesko*
Which tram goes to the museum?	**Który tramwaj jedzie do muzeum?**	*ktoori tramvay yedje do moozeoom*
How many kilometres?	**Ile kilometrów?**	*eele keelometroof*
How long does it take?	**Jak długo?**	*yak dwoogo*

| On foot? | Piechotą? | pyehoto |
| By car? | Samochodem? | samohodem |

You may hear

Skręcić w prawo/ w lewo	skrenchich f pravo/ v levo	Turn right/left
Daleko/blisko	daleko/bleesko	Far/near
Pół godziny piechotą	poow godjeeni pyehoto	Half an hour on foot
Prosto 50 metrów	prosto pyenchdjeshont metroof	Straight on for 50 metres

■ You may enter Poland only at international border crossings. There is an increasing number of these, particularly on the German-Polish border. In addition to a passport, travellers need: the vehicle registration document, their driving licence as well as Green Card – accident insurance which may be purchased at Polish border crossing points.

■ The Polish Motoring Association (**PZM**) has offices at all border crossings. They provide such services as currency exchange and Green Card sales, as well as sales of maps, tourist guides and small souvenirs. They also provide information about travel conditions throughout Poland.

■ Polish roads are marked with international road signs. You drive on the right.

■ The following speed limits are obligatory: 60 km/h in built-up areas, 90 km/h outside built-up areas; 110 km/h on motorways.

■ The motorways and main roads are generally of a reasonable standard, and snow-falls are not an obstacle to driving in Poland, as road maintenance is quite efficient. The smaller roads, on the other hand, vary considerably in standard.

■ Most petrol stations are a part of the CPN chain, but there are now some which are privately-owned. They are usually open from 6 a.m. to 7 p.m. on weekdays, and from 7 a.m. to 3 p.m. on Sundays and holidays, although there are some which offer 24-hour services. Lead-free petrol is available at most larger petrol stations. Premium grade (four-star) petrol and diesel fuel are generally available. An octane numbering system is in use on the petrol pumps, ranging from low-octane 86 to 'Super' 94 or 96.

■ In case of breakdown, there are emergency telephones on motorways and main roads.

■ You can arrange car-hire in Britain with international firms, or in Poland from such companies as Orbis and the Municipal Cab Company in Warsaw, as well as with private firms.

■ If you have to tell a mechanic what's wrong with your vehicle, the easiest way is to indicate the part and say 'This doesn't work': **Nie działa** (*nye djawa*). Otherwise, look up the word in your Dictionary.

You may see

Road signs

Autostrada	Motorway
Daj pierszeństwo przejazdu	Give way
Droga bez wylotu	Cul-de-sac, no through road
Droga zamknięta	Road closed
Niebezpieczeństwo	Danger
Niebezpieczne skrzyżowanie	Dangerous crossing
Niebezpieczny zakręt	Dangerous bend
Nie blokuj wjazdu/wejścia	Do not obstruct the way
Nie ma wjazdu	No entry
Objazd	Diversion
Ograniczenie prędkości	Speed limit
Ostrożnie	Caution
Pierszeństwo z prawej strony	Priority to the right
Powoli or **Wolno**	Slow
Pojazdy ciężarowe	Heavy vehicles
Przejście dla pieszych	Pedestrian crossing
Roboty drogowe	Road works
Ścieżka rowerowa	Cycle path
Skrzyżowanie	Crossing
Skrzyżowanie wielopoziomowe	Level crossing

Stacja benzynowa	Petrol station
Stop	Stop
Strefa dla pieszych	Pedestrian zone
Strzeż się pociągu	Beware of the trains
Szkoła	School
Trzymaj się prawej strony	Keep right
Ulica jednokierunkowa	One-way street
Uwaga	Caution
Włącz światła	Use headlights
Wolno/powoli	Slow
Wyjazd dla pojazdów ciężarowych	Lorry exit
Wyjazd z fabryki/zakładu	Factory exit
Zakaz parkowania	No parking
Zakaz wjazdu	No entry
Zakaz wyprzedzania	No overtaking

Other signs

Bilet parkingowy	Parking ticket (one you buy)	**PKP**	Polish Railways
		Samo-obsługa	Self-service
Centrum	Town/city centre	**Warsztat naprawy samochodów**	Car repairs
Mandat	Fine (penalty)		
Parking strzeżony	Supervised car park	**Wynajmowanie samochodów**	Car hire

You may want to say

At the garage/service station

Is there a petrol station here?	**Czy jest tu stacja benzynowa?**	*chi yest too statsya benzinova*
4-star	**Super**	*sooper*

2-star	**Normalna**	*normalna*
Unleaded petrol	**Bezołowiowa**	*bezowovyova*
Diesel	**Diesel**	*deezel*
20 litres of 4-star, please	**Dwadzieścia litrów super, proszę**	*dvadjeshcha leetroof sooper prosheh*
A can of oil, please	**Puszkę oleju, proszę**	*pooshkeh oleyoo prosheh*
Water, please	**Wody, proszę**	*vodi prosheh*
Can you check the tyres?	**Czy możecie sprawdzić opony?**	*chi mozheche spravdjeech oponi*
Can you clean the window?	**Czy możecie umyć okno?**	*chi mozheche oomich okno*
Where is the air, please?	**Gdzie jest powietrze?**	*gdje yest povyetshe*
How does the car-wash work?	**Jak działa myjnia?**	*yak djawa miynya*
How much is it?	**Ile kosztuje?**	*eele koshtooye*

Parking

Where can I/we park?	**Gdzie można zaparkować?**	*gdje mozhna zaparkovach*
Can I/we park here?	**Można tu zaparkować?**	*mozhna too zaparkovach*
How long can I/we park here?	**Jak długo można tu zaparkować?**	*yak dwoogo mozhna too zaparkovach*
How much is it per hour?	**Ile za godzinę?**	*eele za godjeeneh*

Hiring a car

(see Days, months, dates, page 118)

I want to hire a car	**Chcę wynająć samochód**	*htseh vinayonch samohoot*
A small car, please	**Mały samochód**	*mawi samohoot*
A medium-sized car, please	**Średni samochód**	*shrednee samohoot*

A large car, please	**Duży samochód**	*doozhi samohoot*
An automatic	**Automatyczny samochód**	*awtomatichni samohoot*
For three days	**Na trzy dni**	*na tshi dnee*
For a week	**Na tydzień**	*na tidjen*
For two weeks	**Na dwa tygodnie**	*na dva tigodnye*
From ... to ...	**Od ... do**	*od ... do*
From Monday to Friday	**Od poniedziałku do piątku**	*ot ponyedjawkoo do pyontkoo*
How much is it?	**Ile to kosztuje?**	*eele to koshtooye*
Per day/week?	**Na dzień/tydzień?**	*na djen/tidjen*
Per kilometre?	**Na kilometr?**	*na keelometr*
Is mileage included?	**Czy jest wliczony koszt zużycia?**	*chi yest vleechoni kosht zoozhicha*
Is petrol included?	**Razem z benzyną?**	*razem z benzino*
Is insurance included?	**Razem z ubezpieczeniem?**	*razem z oobespyechenyem*
Comprehensive insurance cover	**Pełne pokrycie ubezpieczeniowe**	*pewne pokriche oobespyechenyove*
My husband/wife is driving too	**Mój mąż/moja żona też prowadzi**	*mooy monsh/moya zhona tesh provadjee*
Can I pay by credit card?	**Czy można zapłacić kartą kredytową?**	*chi mozhna zapwachich karto kreditovo*
Can I pay with traveller's cheques?	**Czy można zapłacić czekami podróżnymi?**	*chi mozhna zapwachich chekamee podroozhn imee*
Can I leave the car at the airport?	**Czy mogę zostawić samochód na lotnisku?**	*chi mogeh zostaveech samohoot na lotneeskoo*
How do the controls work?	**Jak działają kontrolki?**	*yak djawayo kontrolkee*
What kind of petrol does it take?	**Jaką benzynę?**	*yako benzineh*

Breakdowns and repairs

(See Car and bicycle parts, page 30)

My car has broken down	**Samochód mi się zepsuł**	*samohoot mee sheh zepsoow*
This doesn't work	**Nie działa**	*nye djawa*
Is there a garage around here?	**Czy jest blisko warsztat?**	*chi yest bleesko varshtat*
Can you get a mechanic?	**Czy można zawołać mechanika?**	*chi mozhna zavowach mehaneeka*
Can you tow me to a garage?	**Czy możecie pociągnąć mnie do garażu?**	*chi mozheche pochong nonch mnye do garazhoo*
Do you do repairs?	**Czy naprawiacie samochody?**	*chi napravyache samohodi*
I don't know what's wrong	**Nie wiem co się stało**	*nye vyem tso sheh stawo*
I think ...	**Chyba ...**	*hiba*
It's the clutch	**To skrzynia biegów**	*to skshinya byegoof*
It's the radiator	**Chłodnica**	*hwodneetsa*
It's the brakes	**To hamulec**	*to hamoolets*
The car won't start	**Nie chce zapalić**	*nye htse zapaleech*
The battery is flat	**Akumulator nie działa**	*akoomoolator nye djawa*
The engine is overheating	**Silnik przegrzał się**	*sheelneek pshegzhaw sheh*
It's losing oil/water	**Olej/woda wycieka**	*oley/voda vicheka*
It has a puncture	**Przebita dętka**	*pshebeeta dentka*
I don't have any petrol	**Nie mam benzyny**	*nye mam benzini*
I need a ...	**Potrzebuję ...**	*potshebooyeh*
Is it serious?	**To coś poważnego?**	*to tsosh povazhnego*
Can you repair it (today)?	**Można naprawić (dzisiaj)?**	*mozhna napraveech djeeshay*
When will it be ready?	**Kiedy będzie gotowe?**	*kyedi bendje gotove*
How much will it cost?	**Ile będzie kosztować?**	*eele bendje koshtovach*

You may hear

Petrol

Jakiej benzyny?	*yakkey benzini*	What kind of petrol?
Ile?	*eele*	How much?
Kluczyki, proszę	*kloochikee prosheh*	Keys, please

Parking

Tu nie wolno parkować	*too nye volno parkovach*	You can't park here
Bezpłatny	*bespwatni*	It's free
Tam jest parking	*tam yest parking*	The car park is over there

Hiring a car

Jaki samochód chce pan/pani?	*yakee samohoot htse pan/panee*	What kind of car do you want?
Na jak długo?	*na yak dwoogo*	For how long?
Na ile dni?	*na eele dnee*	For how many days?
Prawo jazdy, proszę	*pravo yazdi prosheh*	Driving licence, please

Breakdowns and repairs

Co nie działa?	*tso nye djawa*	What's wrong?
Proszę otworzyć maskę	*prosheh otfozhich maskeh*	Open the bonnet, please
Nie mam tych części	*nye mam tih chenshchee*	I don't have these parts
Będzie gotowy za tydzień	*bendje gotovi za tidjen*	It will be ready in a week's time

Car and bicycle parts

| Accelerator | **Pedał gazu** | *pedaw gazoo* |
| Air filter | **Filtr powietrza** | *feeltr povyetsha* |

30

Alternator	**Alternator**	_alternator_
Battery	**Akumulator**	_akoomoolator_
Bonnet	**Maska**	_maska_
Boot	**Bagażnik**	_bagazhneek_
Brake cable	**Linka hamulca**	_leenka hamooltsa_
Brake fluid	**Płyn hamulca**	_pwin hamooltsa_
Brake hose	**Wąż hamulca**	_vonsh hamooltsa_
Brakes (front/rear)	**Hamulce (przednie/ tylne)**	_hamooltse (pshednye/ tilne)_
Carburettor	**Gaźnik**	_gazhneek_
Chain	**Łańcuch**	_wantsooh_
Clutch	**Sprzęgło**	_spshengwo_
Cooling system	**System chłodzenia**	_sistem hwodzenya_
Distributor	**Rozdzielacz**	_rozdjelach_
Electrical system	**System elektryczny**	_sistem elektrichni_
Engine	**Silnik**	_sheelneek_
Exhaust pipe	**Rura wydechowa**	_roora videhova_
Fan belt	**Pasek klinowy**	_pasek kleenovi_
Frame	**Rama**	_rama_
Fuel gauge	**Paliwomierz**	_paleevomyesh_
Fuel pump	**Pompa paliwowa**	_pompa paleevova_
Fuse	**Bezpiecznik**	_bespyechneek_
Gearbox	**Skrzynia biegów**	_skshinya byegoof_
Gear lever	**Dźwignia**	_dzhveegnya_
Gears	**Biegi**	_byegee_
Handbrake	**Hamulec ręczny**	_hamoolets renchni_
Handlebars	**Kierownica**	_kyerovneetsa_
Headlights	**Reflektory**	_reflektori_
Horn	**Klakson**	_klaxon_
Ignition	**Zapłon**	_zapwon_
Ignition key	**Kluczyk zapłonu**	_kloochik zapwonoo_

Indicator	**Kierunkowskaz**	*kyeroonkofskas*
Inner tube	**Dętka**	*dentka*
Lights (front/rear)	**Światła (przednie/tylne)**	*shfyatwa (pshednye/ tilne)*
Lock	**Zamek**	*zamek*
Oil filter	**Filtr oleju**	*feeltr oleyoo*
Oil gauge	**Miernik oleju**	*myerneek oleyoo*
Pedal	**Pedał**	*pedaw*
Points	**Punkty kontaktów**	*poonkti kontaktoof*
Pump	**Pompa**	*pompa*
Radiator	**Chłodnica**	*hwodneetsa*
Radiator hose	**Wąż chłodnicy**	*vonsh hwodneetsi*
Reversing lights	**Światła cofania**	*shfyatwa tsofanya*
Rotor arm	**Palec rozdzielacza**	*palets rozdjelacha*
Saddle	**Siodło**	*shodwo*
Silencer	**Tłumik**	*twoomeek*
Spare wheel	**Koło zapasowe**	*kowo zapasove*
Spark plugs	**Świeca zapłonowa**	*shfyetsa zapwonova*
Speedometer	**Prędkościomierz**	*prentkoshchomyesh*
Spokes	**Szprychy**	*shprihi*
Starter motor	**Silnik rozruchowy**	*sheelneek rozroohovi*
Steering	**Kierowanie**	*kyerovanye*
Steering wheel	**Kierownica**	*kyeorvneetsa*
Transmission	**Napęd**	*napent*
Tyre	**Opona**	*opona*
Tyre pressure	**Ciśnienie w oponie**	*cheeshnyenye v oponye*
Valve	**Zawór**	*zavoor*
Wheel (front/rear)	**Koło (przednie/tylne)**	*kowo (pshednye/ tilne)*
Windscreen	**Szyba przednia or Okno**	*shiba pshednya/okno*
Windscreen washer	**Spryskiwacz**	*spriskeevach*
Windscreen wiper	**Wycieraczka szyby**	*vicherachka shibi*

Taxis

I If you need a taxi, it is best either to find one at a taxi rank, or phone for one, rather than trying to stop one in the street, especially round the station or the airport. There are different types of taxi, but all of them have a sign on top **Taxi**, **Radio Taxi**, or **Taksówka**.

I Taxis have meters, but it's a good idea to ask what the approximately fare will be, especially if you are going some distance. A tip of 10% is usual.

I Write down clearly the address of your destination if it's complicated. In Polish, addresses are written with the street name first and the number afterwards, e.g. **Aleje Ujazdowskie 59**.

You may want to say

(see also Directions, page 21)

Is there a taxi rank around here?	**Czy jest tu postój taksówek?**	*chi yest too postooy taxoovek*
I need a taxi	**Potrzebuję taksówkę**	*potshebooyeh taxoofkeh*
Can you order me a taxi?	**Czy można zamówić taksówkę?**	*chi mozhna zamooveech taxoofkeh*
Immediately	**Natychmiast**	*natihmyast*
For tomorrow at nine o'clock	**Jutro na dziewiątą**	*yootro na djevyonto*
To the airport, please	**Na lotnisko, proszę**	*na lotneesko prosheh*
To the station, please	**Na stację, proszę**	*na statsyeh prosheh*
To the Forum Hotel, please	**Hotel Forum, proszę**	*hotel forum prosheh*
To this address, please	**Ten adres, proszę**	*ten adres prosheh*
Is it far?	**To daleko?**	*to daleko*

How much will it cost?	**Ile to będzie kosztować?**	*eele to bendje koshtovach*
I'm in a hurry	**śpieszy mi się**	*shpyeshi mee sheh*
Stop here, please	**Proszę tu się zatrzymać**	*prosheh too sheh zatshimach*
Wait a few minutes	**Proszę chwilę zaczekać**	*prosheh hfeeleh zachekach*
There is a mistake	**To pomyłka**	*to pomiwka*
On the meter it says 50 złotys	**Na liczniku jest pięćdziesiąt złotych**	*na leechneekoo yest pyenchdjeshont zwotih*
Keep the change	**Proszę zatrzymać resztę**	*prosheh zatshimach reshteh*
That's all right	**W porządku**	*f pozhontkoo*
Can you give me a receipt?	**Czy mogę prosić o rachunek?**	*chi mogeh prosheech o rahoonek*

You may hear

Dziesięć kilometrów stąd/dziesięć minut stąd	*djeshench keelometroof stont/ djeshench meenoot stont*	It's 10 kilometres away/ 10 minutes from here
Będzie kosztować dziesięć złotych	*bendje koshtovach djeshench zwotih*	It will be ten złotys
Jest dodatek	*yest dodatek*	There is a supplement
Za bagaż	*za bagazh*	For the luggage

Buses and coaches

▌ Normal and express lines on long-distance routes are run by the Polish National Bus Company (**PKS**). You can buy tickets in advance, or on the day of travel, at bus terminals, **Orbis** offices (the main Polish travel agents), as well as from bus drivers, if there are any seats left.

▌ Children under four travel free if they don't occupy a separate seat; children aged from four to ten pay half-fare.

▌ Within the city you can travel on buses, trams and trolley-buses, which are a part of the municipal transportation system. There are normal, shuttle and express lines. Most large cities run local night-time buses.

▌ You can buy tickets at **Ruch** kiosks and some shops. The tickets have to be punched in the machine on the bus as soon as you enter. You have to check in advance exactly how many times you need to punch as prices may change. If you intend to use the buses a lot, you can buy tickets in bulk – coupon books of as many tickets as you want. Ticket prices are dependent on the type of bus service. In Warsaw, you can buy one-day or one-week tickets, but only from one place: the booking office of the Municipal Transport Enterprise (**MZK**), ul. Senatorska 37.

You may see

Autokar	Coach
Dworzec autobusowy	Bus station
Komunikacja miejska	Municipal transportation system
Palenie wzbronione	No smoking
PKS	National Bus Company
Przystanek autobusowy	Bus stop

Przystanek na życzenie   Request stop
Wyjście awaryjne or **zapasowe**   Emergency exit

You may want to say

(for sightseeing bus tours, see Sightseeing, page 83)

Information

Where is the bus stop?	**Gdzie jest przystanek autobusowy?**	*gdje yest pshistanek awtoboosovi*
Where is the bus to the railway station?	**Gdzie jest autobus na stację?**	*gdje yest awtoboos na statsyeh*
What number is the bus to the railway station?	**Który autobus jedzie na stację**	*ktoori awtoboos yedje na statsyeh*
What time is the bus to Zakopane?	**O której jest autobus do Zakopanego?**	*o ktoorey yest awtoboos do zakopanego*
What time does it arrive here?	**O której godzinie przyjeżdża?**	*o ktoorey godjeenye pshiyezhdja*
The next bus	**Następny autobus**	*nastempni awtoboos*
The last bus	**Ostatni autobus**	*ostatnee awtoboos*
Where does the bus to the town centre leave from?	**Skąd odjeżdża autobus do centrum?**	*skont odyezhdja awtoboos do tsentroom*
Does the bus to the airport leave from here?	**Czy stąd odjeżdża autobus na lotnisko?**	*chi stont odyezhdja awtoboos na lotneesko*
I want to get off by the museum	**Chcę wysiąść przy muzeum**	*htse vishonshch pshi moozeoom*
Please tell me where to get off	**Proszę mi powiedzieć gdzie wysiąść**	*prosheh mee povyedjech gdje vishonshch*
The next stop, please	**Następny przystanek**	*nastempni pshistanek*
Excuse me, may I get past?	**Przepraszam**	*psheprasham*

Tickets

One/two to the centre	**Jeden/dwa do centrum**	*yeden/dva do tsentroom*
Where can I buy a multiple ticket?	**Gdzie mogę kupić więcej biletów?**	*gdje mogeh koopeech vyentsey beeletoof*
Twenty tickets, please	**Proszę dwadzieścia biletów**	*prosheh dvadjeshcha beeletoof*
How much is it?	**Ile kosztuje?**	*eele koshtooye*

You may hear

Autobus do centrum odjeżdża z tamtego przystanku	*awtoboos do tsentroom odyezhdja s tamtego pshistankoo*	The bus to the city/town centre leaves from that stop there
Numer cztery jedzie na stację	*noomer chteri yedje na statsyeh*	The number four goes to the station
Jadą co dziesięć minut	*yado tso djeshench meenoot*	They go every 10 minutes
Odjeżdża za pół godziny	*odyezhdja za poow godjeeni*	It leaves in half an hour

37

Travelling by train

■ There are fast and express trains running on international rail links. They have 1st and 2nd class carriages, berths (couchettes), sleepers, and restaurant cars. Most international trains arrive at Warsaw Central Station, which is in the city centre.

■ You can buy tickets at railway stations, through **Orbis** offices (the main Polish travel agents) or other travel agents and from the 'Wagon Lits/Travel' International Society of Sleepers and Tourism. Their prices are based on international ratings.

■ Passenger trains are subdivided into:

local trains – **pociąg osobowy**, which stop at every station, are very slow and not very comfortable;

fast trains – **pociąg pośpieszny**, which stop in larger cities;

express trains – **pociąg ekspresowy**, which stop in major cities only;

Inter-city trains, which stop only at their final destinations;

Eurocity/international trains – **pociąg międzynarodowy**.

■ Tickets are available at PKP (Polish Railways – **Polskie Koleje Państwowe**), booking offices of Orbis and other travel offices. An additional seat reservation is required on all express trains and on some fast trains. You may find that many inter-city trains go either very early in the morning, or late at night, which can be a bit inconvenient.

■ You can buy Polrailpass tickets (non-transferable tickets, valid with a passport, for unlimited trips over certain routes over a specified period of time) at Orbis offices.

■ Left-luggage offices are open 24 hours a day at all major railway stations.

■ Don't rely too much on printed timetables or information boards. If you ask, you may find out about different connecting trains and you can make sure you're getting on the correct train.

■ Work out in advance what you're going to ask for (1st or 2nd class, single or return, adult or child tickets, particular trains, reservations, etc.)

■ Note: you'll notice that sometimes two forms of verbs are used in the phrases – this is because Polish has slightly different verb endings (in the past tense), depending whether the speaker is male or female, and whether it's a man or a woman spoken about. Remember also that when addressing a man you use the form **pan**, but **pani** for a woman.

You may see

Bilety	Tickets
Damski	Women (toilets)
Kasy	Ticket office
Kuszetki	Couchettes
Męski	Men (toilets)
Odbiór bagażu	Baggage reclaim
Odjazdy	Departures
PKP	Polish Railways
Pociągi podmiejskie	Suburban trains
Poczekalnia	Waiting room
Przechowalnia bagażu	Left-luggage office
Przyjazdy	Arrivals
Rozkład jazdy	Timetable
Ubikacje	Toilets
Wagon sypialny	Sleeper
Wejście na perony	Entrance to the platforms
Wyjście (do miasta)	Exit (to town)

Information

(see Time, page 122)

Is there a train to Warsaw?	**Czy jest pociąg do Warszawy?**	*chi yest pochonk do varshavi*
What time?	**O której godzinie?**	*o ktoorey godjeenye*
What time is the train to Zakopane?	**O której godzinie jest pociąg do Zakopanego?**	*o ktoorey godjeenye yest pochonk do zakopanego*
What time does the train from Warsaw arrive?	**O której przyjeżdża pociąg z Warszawy?**	*o ktoorey pshiyezhdja pochonk z varshavi*
Is this the train to Gdańsk?	**Czy to pociąg do Gdańska?**	*chi to pochonk do gdanska*
Which platform does the train to Szczecin leave from?	**Z którego peronu odjeżdża pociąg do Szczecina?**	*s ktoorego peronoo odyezhdja pochonk do shchecheena*
Do I/we have to change trains?	**Czy trzeba się przesiadać?**	*chi tsheba sheh psheshadach*
Where?	**Gdzie?**	*gdje*

Tickets

(see Time, page 122)

One/two to Kraków, please	**Jeden/dwa do Krakowa**	*yeden/dva do krakova*
Single	**W jedną stronę**	*v yedno stroneh*
Return	**Powrotny**	*povrotni*
For one adult/two adults	**Jeden/dwa dla dorosłych**	*yeden/dva dla doroswih*
(And) one child/two children	**(I) jedno dziecko/dwoje dzieci**	*ee yedno djetsko/dvoye djechee*
second/first class	**druga/pierwsza klasa**	*drooga/pyerfsha klasa*

Can I reserve a seat/two seats?	**Czy mogę zarezerwować jedno miejsce/dwa miejsca?**	*chi mogeh zarezervovach yedno myeystse/dva myeystsa*
Can I reserve a sleeper?	**Czy mogę zarezerwować sypialny?**	*chi mogeh zarezervovach sipyalny*
Can I take my bicycle on the train?	**Czy mogę zabrać rower na pociąg?**	*chi mogeh zabrach rover na pochonk*

Left luggage

Can I leave this?	**Czy mogę to zostawić?**	*chi mogeh to zostaveech*
Can I leave these two suitcases?	**Czy mogę zostawić te dwie walizki?**	*chi mogeh zostaveech te dvye valeeski*
Until three o'clock	**Do trzeciej**	*do tshechey*
What time do you close?	**O której zamykacie?**	*o ktoorey zamikache*

On the train

I have reserved a seat	**Zarezerwowałem** (male)/ **zarezerwowałam** (female) **miejsce**	*zarezervovawem/ zarezervovawam myeystse*
Is this seat taken?	**Czy to miejsce zajęte?**	*chi to myeystse zayente*
Do you mind if I open the window?	**Czy można otworzyć okno?**	*chi mozhna otfozhich okno*
Where is the sleeping car?	**Gdzie jest sypialny?**	*gdje yest sipyalny*
Excuse me, may I get past?	**Przepraszam**	*psheprasham*
Do you mind if I smoke?	**Czy można zapalić?**	*chi mozhna zapaleech*
Where are we?	**Gdzie jesteśmy?**	*gdje yesteshmi*
Is this Śląsk?	**Czy jesteśmy na Śląsku?**	*chi yesteshmi na shlonskoo*
How long does the train stop here?	**Jak długo pociąg tu stoi?**	*yak dwoogo pochonk too stoee*

Can you tell me when we get to Nowy Targ?	Czy może pan/pani powiedzieć kiedy dojedziemy do Nowego Targu?	*chi może pan/pani povyedjech kyedi doyedjemi do novego targoo*

You may hear

Information

(see Time, page 122)

Pociąg (do Warszawy) odjeżdża o dziesiątej trzydzieści	*Pochonk (do varshavi) odyezhdja o djeshontey tshidjeshchee*	The train (to Warsaw) leaves at half past ten in the morning
Przyjeżdża o dwudziestej piętnaście	*pshiyezhdja o dvoodjestey pyentnashche*	It arrives at a quarter past eight (in the evening)
Trzeba się przesiąść w Krakowie	*tsheba sheh psheshonshch f krakovye*	You have to change at Kraków
Pociąg (do Katowic) odjeżdża z toru drugiego przy peronie czwartym	*pochonk (do katoveets) odyezhdja s toroo droogyego pshi peronye chfartim*	The train (for Katowice) leaves from platform four, track two

Tickets

(see Time, page 122)

Na kiedy chce pan/pani bilet?	*na kyedi htse pan/panee beelet*	When do you want the ticket for?
Kiedy pan/pani wraca?	*kyedi pan/pani vratsa*	When do you want to return?
Dla palących czy nie palących?	*dla palontsih chi nye palontsih*	Smoking or non-smoking?
Jest tylko pierwsza klasa	*yest tilko pyerfsha klasa*	There's only first class

Air travel

The Polish Airlines company **LOT** maintains regular and seasonal connections with the following major Polish cities: Szczecin, Gdańsk, Poznań, Warszawa, Wrocław, Katowice, Kraków, Rzeszów. You can buy tickets at **LOT** and **Orbis** sales offices.

There is one international airport, called **Okęcie**, which is in Warsaw.

You may see

Damski	Women (toilets)
Lotnisko	Airport
Nic do oclenia	Nothing to declare
Męski	Men (toilets)
Odbiór bagażu	Luggage reclaim
Odlot	Departure
Odprawa (bagażowa/ paszportowa/celna)	Check-in (luggage/ passport/customs)
Opóźnienie	Delay
Palenie wzbronione	No smoking
Port Lotniczy	Airport terminal
Przylot	Arrival
Rzeczy do oclenia	Goods to declare
Ubikacja	Toilet
Wyjście awaryjne or **zapasowe**	Emergency exit
Wyjście do samolotu	Gate
Wymiana pieniędzy	Bureau de change
Wynajmowanie samochodów	Car hire

You may want to say

Is there a flight from Warsaw to Gdańsk?	Czy jest lot z Warszawy do Gdańska?	chi yest lot z varshavi do gdanska
Today	Dzisiaj	djeeshay
This morning/ this afternoon	Dzisiaj rano/po południu	djeeshay rano/po powoodnyoo
Tomorrow (morning/ afternoon)	Jutro (rano/ po południu)	yootro rano/ po powoodnyoo
What time is the first flight to Kraków?	O której jest pierwszy lot do Krakowa?	o ktoorey yest pyerfshi lot do krakova
The next flight	Następny lot	nastempni lot
The last flight	Ostatni lot	ostatnee lot
What time does it arrive (in Warsaw)?	O której przylatuje (do Warszawy)?	o ktoorey pshilatooye do varshavi
A ticket/two tickets to Szczecin	Bilet/dwa bilety do Szczecina	beelet/dva beeleti do shchecheena
Single	W jedną stronę	v yedno stroneh
Return	Powrotny	povrotni
1st class/business class	Pierwsza klasa	pyerfsha klasa
Economy class	Turystyczna	tooristichna
I want to change/ cancel my reservation	Chcę zmienić/ odwołać moją rezerwację	htse zmyeneech/ odvowach moyo rezervatsyeh
What is the flight number?	Jaki jest numer lotu?	yakee yest noomer lotu?
What time do I have to check in?	Kiedy trzeba się zgłosić?	kyedi tsheba sheh zgwosheech?
Which gate is it?	Które wejście?	ktoore veyshche?
Is there a delay?	Czy jest opóźnienie?	chi yest opoozhnyenye?
Where is the luggage from the London flight?	Gdzie jest bagaż z lotu z Londynu?	gdje yest bagazh z lotoo z londinoo
My luggage is not here	Nie ma mojego bagażu	nye ma moyego bagazhoo

| Is there a bus to the town centre? | Czy jest autobus do centrum? | *chi yest awtoboos do tsentroom* |

You may hear

Przy oknie czy w środku?	*pshi oknye chi f shrotkoo*	By the window or in the aisle?
Dla palących czy nie palących?	*dla palontsih chi nye palontsih*	Smoking or non-smoking?
Wejście na pokład nastąpi...	*veyshche na pokwat nastompee*	The flight will board at ...
Kartę wstępu do samolotu, proszę	*karteh fstempoo do samolotoo prosheh*	Boarding pass, please

Announcements you may hear over the airport public address system

Lot do ...	*lot do*	Flight to ...
Odlot	*odlot*	Departure
Opóźnienie	*opoozhnyenye*	Delay
Ostatnie wezwanie	*ostatnye vezvanye*	Last call
Pasażerowie	*pasazherovye*	Passengers
Wyjście numer ...	*viyshche noomer*	Gate number ...

Boats and ferries

■ Coastal and inland trips are available for those interested in sea or river travel. In addition to regular ferry services to and from southern Sweden, excursions are offered by boats sailing between ports on the Baltic coast. You can also make a trip down the Vistula and Odra rivers, or sail through the Mazury Lake district. In some mountain areas you can travel the river by raft.

■ Note: a small boat is called **łódź** (*wooch*), a big one **statek** (*statek*).

You may see

Kabiny	Cabins	**Poduszkowiec**	Hovercraft
Kamizelka	Lifejacket	**Port**	Port
ratunkowa		**Prom**	Ferry
Koło ratunkowe	Lifebelt	**Przystań**	Harbour
Łodzie ratunkowe	Lifeboats	**Wodolot**	Hydrofoil
Molo	Pier	**Zatoka**	Bay

You may want to say

Information

(see Numbers, page 114)

Is there a boat to Świnoujście?	**Czy jest prom do Świnoujścia?**	*chi yest prom do shfeenoooyshcha*
Are there any boat trips?	**Czy są wycieczki łodzią/statkiem?**	*chi so vichechkee wodjo/statkyem*

What time is the boat to Jastarnia?	**O której płynie statek do Jastarni?**	*o ktoorey pwinye statek do yastarnee*
The next boat	**Następny statek**	*nastempni statek*
The last boat	**Ostatni statek**	*ostatnee statek*
What time does it arrive here?	**O której przypływa?**	*o ktoorey pshipwiva*
What time does it return?	**O której wraca?**	*o ktoorey vratsa*
How long is the trip?	**Jak długo trwa wycieczka?**	*yak dwoogo trfa vichechka*
Where can I buy tickets?	**Gdzie mogę kupić bilety?**	*gdje mogeh koopeech beeleti*
Have you got something for sea-sickness?	**Czy mogę dostać coś na chorobę morską?**	*chi mogeh dostach tsosh na horobeh morsko*

Tickets

(see Numbers, page 114)

Four tickets to Kołobrzeg	**Cztery bilety do Kołobrzegu**	*chteri beeleti do kowobzhegoo*
Two adults and two children	**Dwa dla dorosłych i dwa dla dzieci**	*dva dla doroswih ee dva dla djechee*
Single	**W jedną stronę**	*v yedno stroneh*
Return	**Powrotny**	*povrotni*
I want to book tickets for the ferry to Hel	**Chcę zamówić bilety na prom do Helu**	*htse zamooveech beeleti na prom do heloo*
I want to book a cabin	**Chcę zamówić kabinę**	*htse zamoovich kabeeneh*
For one person	**Na jedną osobę**	*na yedno osobeh*
For two people	**Na dwie osoby**	*na dvye osoby*
How much is it?	**Ile to kosztuje?**	*eele to koshtooye*

On board

I have reserved a cabin	**Zarezerwowałem** (male)/ **zarezerwowałam** (female) **kabinę**	*zarezervovawem / zarezervovawam kabeeneh*

| I have reserved two berths | **Zarezerwowałem / zarezerwowałam dwie koje** | *zarezervovawem / zarezervovawam dvye koye* | |
| Where is cabin number 72? | **Gdzie jest kabina siedemdziesiąt dwa?** | *gdje yest kabeena shedemdjeshont dva* | |

You may hear

Wycieczki statkiem we wtorki i w piątki	*vichechkee statkyem ve ftorkee ee f piontkee*	Boat trips on Tuesdays and Fridays
Statek do Darłowa odpływa za pół godziny	*statek do darwova otpwiva za poow godjeeni*	The boat to Darłowo leaves in half an hour
Morze jest wzburzone	*mozhe yest vzboozhone*	The sea is rough
Morze jest spokojne	*mozhe yest spokoyne*	The sea is calm

▌ There are tourist information offices in most towns and cities – look for the sign **Informacja Turystyczna**. Many of the staff speak English.

▌ Tourist information offices have leaflets about sights worth seeing, lists of hotels, town plans and regional maps, and they can supply information about opening times and local transport. They can also book hotel rooms for you.

▌ Note: remember to use the form **pan** when directly addressing a man, and **pani** when addressing a woman.

You may want to say

Where is the tourist information office?	**Gdzie jest informacja turystyczna?**	*gdje yest eenformatsya tooristichna*
Do you speak English?	**Czy mówi pan/pani po angielsku?**	*chi moovee pan/panee po angyelskoo*
Do you have ...?	**Czy ma pan/pani ...?**	*chi ma pan/pani*
Do you have a plan of the town?	**Czy ma pan/pani plan miasta?**	*chi ma pan/panee plan myasta*
Do you have a map of the area?	**Czy ma pan/pani mapę okolicy?**	*chi ma pan/panee mapeh okoleetsi*
Do you have a list of hotels?	**Czy ma pan/pani listę hoteli?**	*chi ma pan/panee leesteh hotelee*
Can you recommend a cheap hotel?	**Czy może pan/pani polecić tani hotel?**	*chi mozhe pan/pani polecheech tanee hotel*
Can you book a hotel for me, please?	**Czy można zarezerwować hotel?**	*chi mozhna zarezervovach hotel*

Can you recommend a traditional restaurant?	**Czy może pan/pani polecić tradycyjną restaurację?**	*chi mozhe pan/ panee polecheech traditsiyno restauratsyeh*
Where can I/we hire a car?	**Gdzie można wynająć samochód?**	*gdje mozhna vinayonch samohoot*
What is there to see here?	**Co tu jest do zobaczenia?**	*tso too yest do zobachenya*
Do you have any information about ...?	**Czy ma pan/pani informację o ...?**	*chi ma pan/panee eenformatsyeh o*
Where is the archaeological museum?	**Gdzie jest muzeum archeologiczne?**	*gdje yest moozeoom arheologeechne*
Can you show me on the map?	**Czy może mi pan/pani pokazać na mapie?**	*chi mozhe mee pan/ panee pokazach na mapye*
When is the museum open?	**Kiedy jest muzeum otwarte?**	*kyedi yest moozeoom otfarte*
Are there any excursions?	**Czy są jakieś wycieczki?**	*chi so yakyesh vichechkee*

You may hear

W czym mogę pomóc?	*f chim mogeh pomoots*	Can I help you?
Skąd pan/pani jest?	*skont pan/panee yest*	Where are you from?
Na jak długo?	*na yak dwoogo*	How long are you staying?
Proszę bardzo	*prosheh bardzo*	Here you are

Accommodation

▌ Hotels in Poland are classified according to a star system, ranging from one to five. Some hotels belong to international hotel chains and prices are comparable to those in other countries. Polish hotels are often managed by travel agencies such as **Orbis SA**, **Syrena**, **Gromada**, **Turysta**, **PTTK**, or run by local tourist enterprises.

▌ The following types of accommodation can be found in Poland:

▌ Inns – **Zajazd** – located along international roads or major domestic roads. Many of them have a regional flavour in both atmosphere and cuisine.

▌ Guest houses – **Pensjonat** – located in popular tourist spots.

▌ **Domy turystyczne** and **Schroniska** (cheaper, more basic) accommodation located along tourist routes and managed by the Polish Society of Touring and Tourism (**PTTK**).

▌ International student hostels – **Międzynarodowe Hotele Studenckie** – managed by the **Almatur** (The Travel and Tourism Bureau of the Polish Students' Association). They offer cheap accommodation in dormitories in the summer months. Holders of valid student IDs can get discounts.

▌ Campsites – **miejsca kampingowe.** They are often affiliated to the Polish Federation of Caravanning and fall into two categories, depending on their standard (I and II). Holders of FICC, AIT and FIA IDs, as well as school pupils and students, get a 10% discount. Children aged four to fourteen get a 20 50% reduction. There are over 200 campsites, located on the outskirts of major cities and in attractive tourist areas. They are indicated by international signs.

▌ Voltage is 220 AC all over Poland.

▌ Note: remember that two verb forms are sometimes used in the phrases. This is because Polish has slightly different verb endings (in the past tense), depending on whether the speaker is male or female, and whether it's a woman or a man being spoken to or referred to. Remember also to use the forms **pan** when addressing a man, and **pani** when addressing a woman.

Information requested on a registration card:

Imię	First name	Miejsce urodzenia	Place of birth
Nazwisko	Surname	Numer paszportu	Passport number
Obywatelstwo	Nationality	Wydany przez	Issued at
Zawód	Occupation	Data	Date
Data urodzenia	Date of birth	Podpis	Signature

You may see

Basen kąpielowy	Swimming pool	Ubikacje	Toilets
Brak wolnych miejsc/pokoi	No vacancies	Windy	Lifts
Dom studencki	Student hostel	Woda nie zdatna do picia	Non-drinking water
Jadalnia	Dining room	Woda zdatna do picia/or pitna	Drinking water
Kamping	Camp site	Wolne miejsca	Vacancies
Łazienka	Bathroom	Wyjście zapasowe or awaryjne	Emergency exit
Namioty	Tents		
Pensjonat	Guest house	Wyżywienie całkowite	Full-board
Pralnia	Laundry		
Prysznic	Showers	Wyżywienie częściowe	Half-board
Recepcja	Reception		
Schronisko górskie	Mountain hut		

Booking in and out

I've reserved a room	**Zarezerwowałem** (male)/ **zarezerwowałam** (female) **pokój**	*zarezervovawem / zarezervovawam pokooy*
My name is ...	**Nazywam się ...**	*nazivam sheh*
Do you have a room?	**Czy jest wolny pokój?**	*chi yest volni pokooy*
A single	**Pokój jednoosobowy**	*pokooy yedno-osobovi*
A double	**Pokój dwuosobowy**	*pokooy dvoo-osobovi*
For one night	**Na jedną noc**	*na yedno nots*
With bath/toilet	**Z łazienką/ubikacją**	*z wazhenko/ oobeekatsyo*
Can I see the room?	**Czy można zobaczyć pokój?**	*chi mozhna zobachich pokooy*
Do you have space for a tent?	**Czy jest miejsce na namiot?**	*chi yest myeystse na namyot*
Do you have space for a caravan?	**Czy jest miejsce na przyczepę kampingową?**	*chi yest myeystse na pshichepeh kampingovo*
How much is it?	**Ile to kosztuje?**	*eele to koshtooye*
Per night	**Za noc**	*za nots*
Per week	**Za tydzień**	*za tidjen*
Is there a reduction for children?	**Czy jest zniżka dla dzieci?**	*chi yest zneeshka dla djechee*
Is breakfast included?	**Razem ze śniadaniem?**	*razem ze shnyadanyem*
It's too expensive	**To za drogo**	*to za drogo*
Do you have anything cheaper?	**Czy jest coś tańszego?**	*chi yest tsosh tanshego*
Do you have anything bigger/smaller?	**Czy jest większy/ mniejszy pokój?**	*chi yest vyenkshi/ mnyeyshi pokooy*
I'd like to stay another night	**Chcę zostać na jeszcze jedną noc**	*htseh zostach na yeshche yedno nots*

I'm leaving tomorrow morning	Wyjeżdżam jutro rano	viyezhdjam yootro rano
The bill, please	Rachunek, proszę	rahoonek prosheh
Do you take credit cards?	Czy przyjmujecie kartę kredytową?	chi pshiymooyeche karteh kreditovo
Do you take traveller's cheques?	Czy przyjmujecie czeki podróżne?	chi pshiymooyeche chekee podroozhne
Can you recommend a hotel in Gdańsk?	Czy może pan/pani polecić hotel w Gdańsku?	chi mozhe pan/ panee polecheech hotel w gdanskoo
Can you phone them to make a booking, please?	Czy może pan/pani zatelefonować i zrobić rezerwację?	chi mozhe pan/ panee zatelefonovach ee zrobeech rezervatsyeh

In hotels

(see Problems and complaints, page 97)

Where can I/we park?	Gdzie można zaparkować?	gdje mozhna zaparkovach
Do you have a cot for the baby?	Czy można dostać łóżeczko dla dziecka?	chi mozhna dostach woozhechko dla djetska
Is there room service?	Czy jest obsługa pokoju?	chi yest opswooga pokoyoo
Do you have facilities for the disabled?	Czy są udogodnienia dla inwalidów?	chi so oodogodnyenya dla eenvaleedoof
What time is breakfast/ dinner?	O której jest śniadanie/ obiad?	o ktoorey yest shnyadanye/obyat
Can I/we have breakfast in the room?	Czy można zjeść śniadanie w pokoju?	chi mozhna zyeshch shnyadanye f pokoyoo
I'll be back very late	Wrócę bardzo późno	vrootseh bardzo poozhno
(Key) number 27	(Klucz) numer dwadzieścia siedem	(klooch) noomer dvadjeshcha shedem
Are there any messages for me?	Czy jest jakaś wiadomość dla mnie?	chi yest yakash vyadomoshch dla mnye
Where is the bathroom?	Gdzie jest łazienka?	gdje yest wazhenka

Can I leave this in the safe?	**Czy mogę zostawić to w sejfie?**	*chi mogeh zostaveech to f seyfye*
Can I have my things from the safe?	**Czy mogę dostać moje rzeczy z sejfu?**	*chi mogeh dostach moye zhechi s seyfoo*
Can you call me at eight o'clock?	**Czy może mnie pan/ pani zawołać o ósmej godzinie?**	*chi mozhe mnye pan/ panee zavowach o oosmey godjeenye*
Can you order me a taxi?	**Czy można zamówić taksówkę?**	*chi mozhna zamooveech taxoofkeh*
For right now	**Na teraz**	*na teras*
For tomorrow at nine o'clock	**Na jutro na dziewiątą**	*na yootro na djevyonto*
Can you find me a babysitter?	**Czy można dostać kogoś do pilnowania dziecka?**	*chi mozhna dostach kogosh do peelnovanya djetska*
Can you put it on the bill?	**Czy można to dodać do rachunku?**	*chi mozhna to dodach do rahoonkoo*
Room number 45	**Pokój numer czterdzieści pięć**	*pokooy noomer chterdjeshchee pyench*

At campsites

Is there a campsite around here?	**Czy jest tu pole kampingowe?**	*chi yest too pole kampeengove*
Can I/we camp here?	**Czy można tu się zatrzymać?**	*chi mozhna too sheh zatshimach*
Where can I/we park?	**Gdzie można zaparkować?**	*gdje mozhna zaparkovach*
Where are the showers?	**Gdzie są prysznice?**	*gdje so prishneetse*
Where are the toilets?	**Gdzie jest ubikacja?**	*gdje yest oobeekatsya*
Where are the dustbins?	**Gdzie są śmieci?**	*gdje so shmyechee*
Is the water drinkable?	**Czy ta woda jest zdatna do picia?**	*chi ta voda yest zdatna do peecha*
Where is the laundry-room?	**Gdzie jest pralnia?**	*gdje yest pralnya*

Where is there an electric point?	**Gdzie jest wtyczka?**	*gdje yest ftichka*

Self-catering accommodation

(see Directions, page 21, and Problems and complaints, page 97)

I have rented a villa	**Wynająłem** (male) / **wynajęłam** (female) **willę**	*vinayowem/ vinayewam veelleh*
I have rented an apartment	**Wynająłem /wynajęłam mieszkanie**	*vinayowem/vinayewam myeshkanye*
We're in number 11	**Jesteśmy pod numerem jedenaście**	*yesteshmi pod noomerem yedenashche*
My name is ...	**Nazywam się ...**	*nazivam sheh*
What is the address?	**Jaki adres?**	*yakee adres*
How do I get there?	**Jak można tam dojść** (on foot) **/dojechać** (in a vehicle)**?**	*yak mozhna tam doyshch/doyehach*
Can you give me the key?	**Czy mogę dostać klucze?**	*chi mogeh dostach klooche*
Where is ...?	**Gdzie jest ...?**	*gdje yest*
Where is the wardrobe?	**Gdzie jest szafa?**	*gdje yest shafa*
Where is the fuse box?	**Gdzie są bezpieczniki?**	*gdje so bespyechneekee*
How does the cooker work?	**Jak działa kuchenka?**	*yak djawa koohenka*
How does the water-heater work?	**Jak działa ogrzewacz wody?**	*yak djawa ogzhevach vodi*
Is there air-conditioning?	**Czy jest klimatyzacja?**	*chi yest kleematizatsya*
Is there a spare gas bottle?	**Czy jest dodatkowa butla gazu?**	*chi yest dodatkova bootla gazoo*
Is there any spare bedding?	**Czy jest dodatkowa pościel?**	*chi yest dodatkova poshchel*
What day do they come to clean?	**Kiedy przychodzi ktoś do sprzątania?**	*kyedi pshihodjee ktosh do spshontanya*

Where do I/we put the rubbish? **Gdzie wyrzucać śmieci?** *gdje vizhootsach shmyechee _*

You may hear

W czym mogę pomóc?	*f chim mogeh pomoots*	Can I help you?
Przepraszam, nie ma wolnych miejsc	*psheprasham nye ma volnih myeysts*	I'm sorry, we're full
Na ile dni?	*na eele dnee*	For how many days?
Na ile osób?	*na eele osoop*	For how many people?

■ Telecommunications in Poland are not yet as efficient as in Britain. Major cities and tourist centres have automatic telephone connections but to telephone to or from a smaller place you may need operator-assisted calls, or you might have to go to the post office. Post offices are usually open from 8 a.m. to 8 p.m on weekdays. The opening hours are shorter on Saturdays, and on Sundays most post offices are closed, except for Voivodship (county) capitals, which have a post office open 24 hours a day. Main post offices have telex and fax facilities; some hotels also offer fax facilities.

■ Most of the newer public phones in the street are for phonecards, which you can buy at post offices. They have **Karta Telefoniczna** written on them.

■ You will have to check whether you need to use coins or a **żeton** (a plastic token you can get at post offices) in the public phone.

Instructions you may see in the phone box

Odbierz kartę	Take out the card
Poczekaj na sygnał	Wait until you hear the dialling tone
Podnieś słuchawkę	Lift the receiver
Włóż kartę	Insert the card
Wrzuć żeton (or **monetę**)	Insert 'żeton' (or coin)
Wykręć numer	Dial the number

You may see

Książka telefoniczna	Telephone directory
Nieczynny	Out of order
Numer kodu	Area code
Rozmowa lokalna	Local call
Rozmowa międzymiastowa	Long-distance call
Rozmowa międzynarodowa	International call

You may want to say

(See also Numbers, page 114)

Where is the telephone?	**Gdzie jest telefon?**	*gdje yest telefon*
Do you chave change for the telephone, please?	**Czy ma pan/pani drobne na telefon?**	*chi ma pan/panee drobne na telefon*
Do you have a telephone directory?	**Czy jest książka telefoniczna?**	*chi yest kshonshka telefoneechna*
I want to call England	**Chcę zadzwonić do Anglii**	*htse zadzvoneech do anglee*
Extension number 127, please	**Numer wewnętrzny sto dwadzieścia siedem**	*noomer vevnentshni sto dvadjeshcha shedem*
My name is ...	**Nazywam się ...**	*nazivam sheh*
It's ... speaking	**Mówi ...**	*moovee*
When will he/she be back?	**Kiedy on/ona wróci?**	*kyedi on/ona vroochi*
I'll call again later	**Zadzwonię później**	*zadzvonyeh poozhnyey*
Can I leave a message?	**Czy mogę zostawić wiadomość?**	*chi mogeh zostaveech vyadomoshch*
Please tell him/her that I called	**Proszę jemu/jej powiedzieć że dzwoniłem** (male)/ **dzwoniłam** (female)	*proshe yemoo/yey povyedjech zhe dzvoneewem/ dzvoneewam*

59

I'm at the Solec Hotel	Jestem w hotelu Solec	*yes*tem f *hoteloo solets*
I'll wait	Zaczekam	*zachekam*
My telephone number is ...	Mój numer jest ...	*mooy noomer yest*
Can you ask him/her to call me back?	Niech zadzwoni później	*nyeh zadzvonee poozhnyey*
Can you repeat that, please?	Czy może pan/pani powtórzyć?	*chi mozhe pan/panee poftoozhich*
More slowly, please	Powoli, proszę	*povolee prosheh*
Sorry, I've got the wrong number	Przepraszam, pomyłka	*psheprasham pomiwka*
We've been cut off	Przerwano połączenie	*pshervano powonchenye*
How much is the call?	Ile kosztuje rozmowa?	*eele koshtooye rozmova*

You may hear

Słucham?	*swooham*	Hello? (said by person answering the phone)
Przy telefonie	*pshi telefonye*	Speaking
Chwileczkę, już łączę	*hfeelechke yooosh woncheh*	One moment, I'm putting you through
Linia zajęta	*leenya zajenta*	The line is engaged

Eating and drinking

(See also Menu reader, page 67)

▌ There are three main meals in Poland: breakfast – **śniadanie**, lunch – **obiad**, which in Poland is the main meal of the day, and supper – **kolacja** – usually smaller and lighter than **obiad**.

▌ All major hotels and tourist facilities have restaurants. Larger hotel restaurants may serve foreign dishes in addition to Polish cuisine. There is an increasing number of specialist restaurants serving oriental (especially Chinese and Vietnamese) food. The larger cities offer the widest selection.

▌ Bills which do not include service say: '**obsługa niewliczona**'.

▌ A tip of 10% is normal.

▌ In most restaurants, in addition to a menu, there is usually a set-price three course meal, called **zestaw firmowy**.

▌ If you are a vegetarian, you can get a moderately-priced meal in milk-bars – **bar mleczny** – which serve dishes based on milk and dairy products, as well as on vegetables. Milk-bars do not serve alcohol.

▌ Cafés – **kawiarnia** – serve coffee, tea, cold drinks, alcoholic beverages, pastries and desserts. Hotel cafés generally serve breakfast, too. Coffee is usually the espresso type, served black or with milk or cream. Tea is always served black or with lemon; you have to ask for milk separately.

▌ Fast-food bars – **jedzenie szybkiej obsługi** – offer pizzas, hamburgers, hot dogs, etc.; there is a growing number of 'McDonalds' and 'Burger Kings'. These exist alongside the street stalls selling traditional Polish delicacies, like **zapiekanki** – small fried snacks.

▌ There are also seafood restaurants – **restauracja rybna** – often slightly cheaper than ordinary restaurants.

There some pubs in Poland (called **pub**). They vary in standard, from the expensive elegant ones to really basic. They are often open until late at night and offer a great variety of good beers. In addition to pubs there are plenty of bars catering for all tastes, ranging from cheap roadside huts to expensive nightclub-style venues. Many bars serve hot food and small snacks.

There is also a well-developed summertime pavement café culture.

You may see

Bar mleczny	Milk-bar
Dania rybne	Fish dishes
Dla pań/ **Dla panów**	Ladies/ Gentlemen
Jadłospis	Menu
Jedzenie szybkiej obsługi	Fast food
Jedzenie zdrowotne	Health food
Karta dań	Menu
Kawiarnia	Café
Kuchnia	Kitchen/Cuisine
Napoje alkoholowe	Alcoholic drinks
Napoje bezalkoholowe	Soft drinks
Przyjmujemy karty kredytowe	We accept credit cards
Restauracja dietetyczna	Health-food restaurant
Restauracja rybna	Fish restaurant
Samo-obsługa	Self-service
Szatnia or **Garderoba**	Cloakroom
Toalety	Toilets
Winiarnia	Wine bar
Zapiekanka	Small fried snack

You may want to say

General phrases

Are there any inexpensive restaurants around here? **Czy są tu jakieś tanie restauracje?** *chi so too yakyesh tanye restauratsye*

A ... please	Raz ... proszę	ras prosheh
Two of these, please	Dwa razy ... proszę	dva razi prosheh
Another one, please	Jeszcze jedno proszę	yeshche yedno prosheh
For me	Dla mnie	dla mnye
For him/her (formal)	Dla pana/pani	dla pana/panee
This one, please	To, proszę	to prosheh
More ..., please	Więcej ..., proszę	vyentsey prosheh
Do you have ...?	Czy macie ...?	chi mache ...
Is/are there any ...?	Czy jest/są ...?	chi yest/so ...
What is there for dessert?	Co jest na deser?	tso yest na deser
What do you recommend?	Co polecacie?	tso poletsache
Do you have any typical local dishes?	Czy jest jakieś danie typowe dla tego regionu?	chi yest yakyesh danye tipove dla tego regyonoo
What is this?	Co to jest?	tso to yest
Cheers!	Na zdrowie	na zdrovye
Enjoy your meal!	Smacznego!	smachnego
Nothing else, thanks	To wszystko, dziękuję	to fshistko djenkooyeh
The bill, please	Rachunek, proszę	rahoonek prosheh
Where are the toilets?	Gdzie jest ubikacja?	gdje yest oobeekatsya

In cafés and fast-food restaurants

A black coffee, please	Czarną Kawę	charno kaveh prosheh
With milk/cream	Z mlekiem/ ze śmietaną	z mlekyem/ze shmyetano
Two teas, please	Dwie herbaty, proszę	dvye herbati prosheh
A tea with milk/lemon	Herbata z mlekiem/z cytryną	herbata z mlekyem/s tsitrino
Herbal tea, please	Herbata ziołowa, proszę	herbata zhowova prosheh
Mineral water, please	Wodę mineralną, proszę	vodeh meeneralno prosheh
Fizzy/still	Z gazem/bez gazu	z gazem/bez gazoo
What fruit juices do you have?	Jakie są soki owocowe?	yakye so sokee ovotsove

An orange juice, please	**Sok pomarańczowy, proszę**	*sok pomaranchovi prosheh*
A beer, please	**Piwo, proszę**	*peevo prosheh*
Two draught beers, please	**Dwa piwa beczkowe proszę**	*dva peeva bechkove prosheh*
A glass of red wine, please	**Kieliszek czerwonego wina, proszę**	*kyeleeshek chervonego veena prosheh*
Dry/sweet	**Wytrawne/słodkie**	*vitravne/swotkye*
With ice	**Z lodem**	*z lodem*
What sandwiches do you have?	**Jakie macie kanapki?**	*yakye mache kanapkee*
A ham sandwich, please	**Kanapkę z szynką, proszę**	*kanapkeh s shinko prosheh*
Two cheese sandwiches, please	**Dwie kanapki z serem**	*dvye kanapki s serem*
Do you have ice cream?	**Czy są lody?**	*chi so lodi*
Chocolate/vanilla, please	**Czekoladowe/ waniliowe, proszę**	*chekoladove/ vaneelyove prosheh*

Booking a table

I want to reserve a table for two people	**Chcę zamówić stolik na dwie osoby**	*htse zamooveech stoleek na dvye osobi*
For eight o'clock	**Na ósmą**	*na oosmo*
For tomorrow at half past six	**Na jutro na szóstą trzydzieści**	*na yootro na shoosto tshidjeshchee*
I have reserved a table	**Mam zarezerwowany stolik**	*mam zarezervovani stoleek*
The name is ...	**Nazwisko ...**	*nazveesko*

In restaurants

A table for four, please	**Stolik na cztery osoby**	*stoleek na chtery osobi*
Outside/on the terrace, if possible	**Na zewnątrz/na tarasie, jeżeli możliwe**	*na zevnontsh/na tarashe yezhelee mozhleeve*

Waiter/waitress!	Proszę pana/Proszę pani	prosheh pana/prosheh panee
The menu, please	Proszę menu/kartę	prosheh menoo/karteh
Do you have a set menu?	Czy jest zestaw firmowy?	chi yest zestaf feermovi
Do you have vegetarian dishes?	Czy są dania bezmięsne/jarskie?	chi so danya bezmyensne/yarskye
The wine list, please	Proszę listę win	prosheh leesteh veen
What hors d'oeuvres do you have?	Jakie macie przekąski?	yakye mache pshekonskee
For the main course ...	Na drugie danie ...	na droogye danye ...
Pork cutlet, please	Kotlet schabowy, proszę	kotlet shabovi prosheh
Does that come with vegetables?	Czy to razem z jarzynami?	chi to razem z yazhinamee
With chips	Z frytkami	s fritkamee
With salad	Z sałatką	s sawatko
For dessert ...	Na deser ...	na deser ...
A piece of cheesecake, please	Sernik, proszę	serneek prosheh
Mixed fruit ice-cream, please	Lody owocowe, proszę	lodi ovotsove prosheh
With cream, please	Z kremem, proszę	s kremem prosheh
What cheeses are there?	Jakie są sery?	yakye so seri
More bread, please	Więcej chleba, proszę	vyentsey hleba prosheh
A glass/jug of water, please	Szklankę/dzbanek wody, proszę	shklankeh/dzbanek vodi prosheh
A bottle of (your) red house wine	Butelkę czerwonego domowego wina	bootelkeh chervonego domovego veena
Half a bottle of white wine	Pół butelki białego wina	poow bootelkee byawego veena
It's very good	Bardzo dobre	bardzo dobre
This is burnt	To jest spalone	to yest spalone

This is not cooked	**To jest niedogotowane**	*to yest nyedogotovane*
No, I ordered chicken	**Nie, zamówiłem** (male)/ **zamówiłam** (female) **kurczaka**	*nye zamooveewem/ zamooveewam koorchaka*
The bill, please	**Rachunek, proszę**	*rahoonek prosheh*
Is service included?	**Razem z obsługą?**	*razem z opswoogo*
Do you accept credit cards?	**Czy przyjmujecie kartę kredytową?**	*chi pshiymooyeche karteh kreditovo*
Do you accept traveller's cheques?	**Czy przyjmujecie cheki podróżne?**	*chi pshiymooyeche chekee podroozhne*
Excuse me, there is a mistake	**Przepraszam, tu jest pomyłka**	*psheprasham too yest pomiwka*

You may hear

In cafés and fast-food restaurants

Co podać?	*tso podach*	What would you like?
Czy podać coś do picia?	*chi podach tsosh do peecha*	Would you like a drink?
Na zimno czy na gorąco?	*na zheemno chi na gorontso*	Hot or cold?
Już podaję	*yoosh podayeh*	Right away

Restaurants

Ile osób?	*eele osoop*	How many of you are there?
Czy zarezerwowany stół?	*chi zarezervovani stoow*	Have you reserved a table?
Coś jeszcze?	*tsosh yeshche*	Anything else?
Obsługa niewliczona	*opswooga nyevleechona*	Service not included

(See also Eating and drinking, page 61)

General phrases

Aperitify	Apéritifs	Łącznie z podatkiem VAT	VAT included
Dania bezmięsne	Vegetarian dishes	Menu	Menu
Dania rybne	Fish dishes	Mięso	Meat
Dania z jaj	Egg dishes	Napoje alkoholowe	Alcoholic drinks
Danie dnia	Dish of the day	Napoje bezalkoholowe	Non-alcoholic drinks
Deser	Dessert	Napoje chłodzące	Cold drinks
Drób	Poultry	Obiad	Dinner (main meal of the day)
Dziczyzna	Game		
Herbata	Tea	Obsługa (niewliczona)	Service (not included)
Jadalnia	Dining room		
Jadłospis	Menu	Owoce	Fruit
Jarzyny	Vegetables	Owoce morza	Seafood
Jedzenie domowe	Home cooking	Piwo	Beer
Jedzenie szybkiej obsługi	Fast food	Porcja	Portion
Kanapki	Sandwiches	Przekąski	Starters/Snacks
Karta dań	Menu	Sałatki	Salads
Kawa	Coffee	Sery	Cheeses
Kelner/Kelnerka	Waiter/Waitress	Szef kuchni poleca	Recommended by the chef
Kolacja	Supper		
Kuchnia	Cuisine	Śniadanie	Breakfast
Lista cen	Price list		

Wina (białe, czerwone, wytrawne, pół wytrawne, słodkie)	Wines (white, red, dry, demi-sec, sweet)
Woda mineralna	Mineral water
Zestaw dnia/Zestaw firmowy	Set menu
Zupy	Soups

Drinks

Alkohole	Alcoholic drinks	Mleko	Milk
Czekolada (gorąca/zimna)	Chocolate (hot/cold)	Napoje	Drinks
Gin	Gin	Piwo	Beer
Herbata	Tea	beczkowane	draught
miętowa	peppermint	ciemne	dark
rumiankowa	camomile	jasne	lager
z cytryną/bez cytryny	with lemon/ without lemon	z butelki	bottled
ziołowa	herbal	Sok	Juice
z mlekiem/bez mleka	with milk/ without milk	grejpfrutowy	grapefruit juice
Jabłecznik	Cider	jabłkowy	apple juice
Kawa	Coffee	pomarańczowy	orange juice
biała/czarna	white/black	pomidorowy	tomato juice
bez kafeiny	decaffeinated	z czarnej porzeczki	blackcurrant juice
ze śmietanką	... with cream	Szampan	Champagne
Kefir	Sour milk	Wermut	Vermouth
Koktajle	Cocktails	Winiak	Polish cognac
Koniak	Cognac	Wino	Wine
Likier	Liqueur	białe	white wine
Lód (z lodem/bez lodu)	Ice (with ice/without ice)	czerwone	red wine
		domowe	house wine
		pół-wytrawne	demi-sec wine
		słodkie	sweet wine

stołowe	table wine	Wódka	Vodka
Woda	Water	czysta	be...
gazowana/	fizzy/	wyborowa	vod...
bez gazu	still water	cytrynówka	lemon vo...
mineralna	mineral water	jarzębiak	rowan vodka
sodowa	soda water	pejsachówka	Jewish vodka
stołowa	table water	wiśniówka	cherry vodka
źródlana	spring water	żubrówka	vodka with a blade of grass
		żytnia	rye vodka

Food

Barszcz	Beetroot soup	Bryzol	Beef steak (thinner, cheaper cut)
czerwony	red		
zabielany	with sour cream	Budyń	Custard-type dessert
z uszkami	with paté meatballs		
Befsztyk	Beef steak (best cut)	Bukiet z jarzyn	Mixed vegetable dish
tatarski	raw minced beef with seasoning	Bułka	Bread roll
z polędwicy	sirloin steak	Buraczki	Grated boiled beetroot
Bezy	Meringue	Chleb	Bread
Bigos	Traditional hunter's dish, with sauerkraut and meat	Chłodnik	Cold soup
		Ciastko	Small pastry cake
		Ciasto	Cake
		Cielęcina	Veal
Bita śmietana	Whipped cream	Comber barani	Saddle of mutton
Botwinka	Beetroot soup made with young beet	Fasola po bretońsku	Baked beans
Brukselka	Brussels sprouts	Fasola szparagowa	French beans

...cy	Veal escalope	Kisiel	Jelly-type dessert
...ki cielęce	Veal tripe	Klopsiki or	Meatballs in
Frytki	Chips	pulpety w sosie	tomato/ mushroom
Galaretka owocowa	Fruit jelly	pomidorowym/ grzybowym	sauce
Gęś pieczona	Roast goose	Kluski	Noodles
Golonka	Cured and boiled ham on the bone	Kompot	Stewed fruit
		Kopytka	Potato dumplings
Gołąbki	Meat and rice wrapped in cabbage leaves	Korniszony	Gherkins
		Kotlet	Meat cutlet/chop
		cielęcy	veal chop
Grzyby	Mushrooms	mielony	fried minced meat with onions
Gulasz	Goulash		
Jajko	Egg	schabowy	pork chop fried in batter
gotowane na miękko/	soft-boiled		
		Kurczak	Chicken
gotowane na twardo	hard-boiled	pieczony	roast
		w potrawce	in sour cream sauce
sadzone	fried		
Jajecznica	scrambled eggs	z rożna	barbecued
Jajka faszerowane	stuffed eggs	Kuropatwa	Partridge
		Lody	Ice cream
Jarzynowa	Vegetable soup	waniliowe	vanilla ice cream
Kaczka pieczona z jabłkami	Duck roasted with apples	owocowe	mixed fruit ice cream
Kanapka	Sandwich	czekoladowe	chocolate ice cream
Kapusta kiszona	Sauerkraut		
Kapuśniak	Cabbage soup	Łosoś	Salmon
Karp w galarecie	Carp in aspic	Makowiec	Poppy-seed cake
Kartoflanka	Potato soup	Masło	Butter
Kasza gryczana	Roasted buckwheat	Mizeria	Cucumber in sour cream
Kiełbasa	Sausage	Nadzienie	Stuffing

70

Naleśniki z serem i ze śmietaną	Pancakes with curd cheese and cream	**Rumsztyk**	Rump steak
		Ryba	Fish
		Ryż	Rice
Nóżki w galarecie	Pig's trotters in aspic	**Sałata**	Lettuce
Ogórki kiszone	Sour cucumbers (in brine)	**Sałatka** or **Surówka**	Salad
Omlet	Omelette	**Schab pieczony**	Roast pork loin
Parówki	Frankfurters	**Sernik**	Cheesecake
Pasztet (z zająca)	Paté (made from hare)	**Sery**	Cheeses
		biały	curd cheese
Pieczarki smażone	Fried mushrooms	**żółty**	hard cheese
		topiony	processed cheese
Pieczeń	Roast	**Śledź**	Herring
cielęca	veal	**w śmietanie**	in sour cream
wieprzowa	pork	**w oliwie**	in oil
wołowa	beef	**Sos**	Sauce
Pieczywo	Bread, rolls, croissants, etc.	**koperkowy**	dill sauce
		grzybowy	mushroom sauce
Pierogi	Stuffed pasta	**pomidorowy**	tomato sauce
z mięsem	with meat	**Stek**	Steak
leniwe (rosyjskie)	with curd cheese and cream	**Surówka** or **Sałatka**	Salad
z kapustą i grzybami	with cabbage and mushrooms	**Szarlotka**	Apple charlotte
		Szaszłyk	Kebab
z jagodami	with bilberries	**Sznycel cielęcy**	Wiener schnitzel
Placki ziemniaczane	Potato pancakes	**Sztuka mięsa w sosie chrzanowym**	Boiled beef with horseradish sauce
Pstrąg z wody	Poached trout		
Rolmops	Pickled herring	**Szynka**	Ham
Rosół z makaronem	Clear chicken soup with noodles	**gotowana**	boiled
		wędzona	smoked
Rozbef	Roast beef	**golonka**	cured on the bone

71

Tort	Gateau
mokka	coffee gateau
czekoladowy	chocolate gateau
owocowy	fruit gateau
orzechowy	nut gateau
Twarożek	Cottage cheese
Węgorz wędzony	Smoked eel
Wieprzowina	Pork
Zając w śmietanie	Hare in cream sauce
Ziemniaki	Potatoes
puree	mashed potatoes
w mundurkach	jacket potatoes
Zrazy zawijane	Rolled beef, filled with stuffing
Zupa	Soup
jarzynowa	vegetable soup
grzybowa	mushroom soup
owocowa	fruit soup
pomidorowa	tomato soup
szczawiowa	sorrel soup
Żeberka	Spare ribs
Żur z kiełbasą	Sour rye soup with sausage

Business trips

▋ You'll probably be doing business with the help of interpreters or in a language everyone speaks, but you may need a few Polish phrases to cope at a company's reception desk.

▋ When you arrive for an appointment, all you need to say is who you've come to see, and give your name or hand over your business card. However, if you are not expected, you may need to make an appointment or leave a message.

▋ Make sure you use the appropriate distinction **pan/pani** (Mr/Mrs) depending on whether you are addressing a man (**pan**) or a woman (**pani**).

▋ Note: remember there are different verbal and adjectival endings depending on whether it's a man or a woman speaking (or being spoken about).

You may see

Firma	Firm/company
Nieczynna	Out of order (lift)
Nie działa	Out of order
Parter	Ground floor
I piętro	1st floor
II piętro	2nd floor
Prosimy nie palić	No smoking
Przedsiębiorstwo	Firm/company
Spółka z ograniczoną odpowiedzialnością/'Sp.z.o.o.'	Limited liability company
Wejście	Entrance
Wejście tylko dla upoważnionych	Entrance for authorized persons only

Winda	Lift
Wyjście	Exit
Wyjście awaryjne or zapasowe	Emergency exit

You may want to say

(see also Days, months, dates, page 118, and Time, page 122)

My name is ...	**Nazywam się ...**	*nazivam sheh*
I work for ...	**Jestem z firmy ...**	*yestem s feermi*
I have an appointment with...	**Jestem umówiony** (male)/**umówiona** (female) **panem/ z panią ...**	*yestem oomoovyoni/ oomoovyona s panem/s panyo*
I'd like to make an appointment with Mr Wojciechowski/ Mrs Wojciechowska, please	**Chciałbym** (male) **chciałabym** (female) **umówić się z panem Wojciechowskim** (Mr)/ **z panią Wojciechowską** (Mrs or Miss)	*hchawbim/hchawabim oomooveech sheh s panem voychehofskeem/ s panyo voychehofsko*
I'd like to talk to the export manager	**Chciałbym** (male) / **chciałabym** (female) **rozmawiać z kierownikiem eksportu**	*hchawbim /hchawabim rozmavyach s kyerovneekyem exportoo*
What's his/her name?	**Jak on/ona się nazywa?**	*yak on/ona sheh naziva*
When will he/she be back?	**Kiedy on/ona wróci?**	*kyedi on/ona vroochee*
Can I leave a message?	**Czy mogę zostawić wiadomość?**	*chi mogeh zostaveech vyadomoshch*
Can you tell him/her to call me?	**Proszę mu/jej powiedzieć, żeby zadzwonił** (male)/ **zadzwoniła** (female)	*prosheh moo/yey povyedjech zhebi zadzvoneew / zadzvoneewa*
My telephone number is ...	**Mój numer telefonu ...**	*mooy noomer telefonoo*

I'm staying at the Metropol Hotel	Jestem w Hotelu Metropol	*yestem f hoteloo metropol*
Where is his/her office?	Gdzie jest jego/jej pokój?	*gdje yest yego/yey pokooy*
I'm here for the conference	Jestem tu na konferencji	*yestem too na konferentsee*
I'm attending the exhibition	Jestem na wystawie	*yestem na vistavye*
I have to make a phone call (to Britain)	Muszę zadzwonić (do Anglii)	*moosheh zadzvoneech do anglee*
I have to send a telex	Muszę wysłać teleks	*moosheh viswach teleks*

You may hear

Pana (male)/pani (female) nazwisko?	*pana/panee nazveesko*	Your name, please?
Z jakiej pan/pani jest firmy?	*z yakyey pan/panee yest feermi*	Which firm do you work for?
Proszę usiąść i zaczekać	*prosheh ooshonshch ee zachekach*	Please sit down and wait
Dyrektor jest na zebraniu	*direktor yest na zebranyoo*	The director is in a meeting

75

Shopping

▌ The majority of grocery shops (**sklep spożywczy**) are open on weekdays from 6 a.m. to 7 p.m., and on Saturdays from 7 a.m. to 1 p.m. Smaller shops usually have more variable opening hours. On Sundays, public holidays and at night, certain selected food-stores are open in the big cities.

▌ Other shops and services are open on weekdays from approximately 11 a.m. to 7 p.m. On Saturdays the opening hours are shorter.

▌ Department stores are usually open on weekdays from 9 a.m. to 8 p.m; on Saturdays the opening hours are slightly shorter.

▌ Most shops and services are closed on Sundays.

▌ Gift shops are open from 11 a.m. to 7 p.m. Of these, the most popular are: **Cepelia**, selling traditional handicrafts;

   Jubiler and **Orno** shops, specializing in silver jewellery;

   Desa shops and private art galleries, selling works of art.

▌ Imported foodstuffs and manufactured goods are sold in **Pewex** and **Baltona** stores, as well as in some private shops. The stores are usually open on weekdays from 8 a.m. to 8 p.m. in city centres; in smaller places, they are open from 11 a.m. to 7 p.m.

▌ **Apteka** shops sell mainly medicines and pharmaceutical products, as well as some toiletries and, sometimes, health foods.

▌ **Drogeria** are shops which sell soap and cleaning products; toiletries and cosmetics are sold in both **Perfumeria** and in **Drogeria**. However, these shops do not sell medicines.

▌ All big cities have a few department stores – **Dom towarowy**; otherwise, Polish shops tend to be small and specialized.

▌ Cigarettes are sold at **Kiosk** news-stands, as well as in grocery shops. There are also tobacconists – **Sklep z wyrobami**

tytoniowymi – selling tobacco, pipes and all the smoker's para-phernalia.

❚ Note: notice the forms **pan** (Mr) or **pani** (Mrs, Ms), when directly addressing people.

Types of shops

Antyki	Antiques
Antykwariat	Second-hand bookshop
Apteka	Chemist (mainly medicines)
Artykuły elektryczne	Electrical goods shop
Artykuły gospodarstwa domowego	Hardware shop
Centrum handlowe	Shopping centre
Cepelia	Craft shop
Cukiernia	Cake shop
Dom towarowy	Department store
Drogeria	Chemist (without pharmacy)
Fryzjer	Hairdressers
Galanteria (damska/męska)	Clothes shop (for women/men)
Garmażeria	Cold meats shop
Jubiler	Jeweller's
Komis	Second-hand shop
Konfekcja (damska/męska)	Clothes shop (for women/men)
Księgarnia	Bookshop
Kwiaciarnia	Flower shop
Meble	Furniture shop
Mleczarnia	Milk and dairy products
Muzyczny (sklep)	Music shop

Obuwie	Shoe shop
Odzież (damska/męska)	Clothes shop (for women/men)
Optyczny (sklep)	Optician
Pamiątki	Souvenirs
Papeteria	Stationer
Pasmanteria	Haberdashery
Perfumeria	Chemist (selling toiletries/ cosmetics without pharmacy)
Piekarnia	Baker
Poczta	Post office
Pralnia chemiczna	Dry-cleaner
Ruch kiosk	News-stand
Rybny (sklep)	Fishmonger
Rzeźnik	Butcher
Samo-obsługowy (sklep)	Self-service (shop)
Sklep	Shop
Sklep z wyrobami tytoniowymi	Tobacconist
Skórzany	Leather goods shop
Słodycze	Sweet shop
Sportowy	Sports shop
Spożywczy (sklep)	Grocer
Szewc	Shoe repairs
Upominki	Souvenirs
Warzywa	Greengrocer
Wyroby skórzane	Leather goods shop
Zabawki	Toy shop
Zegarmistrz	Watchmaker

Other items

Buty	Shoes	Przymierzalnia	Fitting room
Kasa	Cash desk	Wejście	Entrance
Otwarty	Open	Wędliny	Cold meats
Owoce	Fruit	Wyjście	Exit
Mięso	Meat	Wyprzedaż	Sale
Nieczynne	Closed or Out of order	Zamknięty	Closed
Pieczywo	Bread, rolls, croissants, etc.	Żywność or Jedzenie	Food

You may want to say

General phrases

(see also Directions, page 21)

Where is the main shopping area?	Gdzie jest główne centrum handlowe?	gdje yest **gwoov**ne **tsent**room hand**lo**ve
Where is the chemist (for medicines)?	Gdzie jest apteka?	gdje yest ap**te**ka
Is there a grocer's shop around here?	Czy jest blisko sklep spożywczy?	chi yest **blees**ko sklep spozhif**chi**
Where can I buy batteries?	Gdzie mogę kupić baterie?	gdje **mo**geh **koo**peech ba**te**rye
What time does the bakery open?	O której otwierają piekarnię?	o **ktoo**rey otfye**ra**yo pye**kar**nyeh
What time does the post office close?	O której zamykają pocztę?	o **ktoo**rey zami**ka**yo **poch**teh
What time do you open in the morning?	O której otwieracie rano?	o **ktoo**rey otfye**ra**che **ra**no
What time do you close this evening?	O której zamykacie wieczorem?	o **ktoo**rey zami**ka**che vye**cho**rem
Do you have ...?	Czy jest (singular)/ są (plural) ...?	chi yest/so ...

Do you sell stamps?	Czy są znaczki?	*chi so znachkee*
How much is it?	Ile kosztuje?	*eele koshtooye*
Altogether	Razem	*razem*
I don't understand	Nie rozumiem	*nye rozoomyem*
Can you write it down, please?	Czy może pan/pani to napisać?	*chi mozhe pan/ panee to napeesach*
It's too expensive	Za drogo	*za drogo*
Have you got anything cheaper?	Czy jest coś tańszego?	*chi yest tsosh tanshego*
I don't have enough money	Nie mam tyle pieniędzy	*nye mam tile pyenyendzi*
Can you keep it for me?	Czy może pan/pani to dla mnie zatrzymać?	*chi mozhe to pan/panee dla mnye zatshimach*
I'm just looking	Tylko patrzę	*tilko patsheh*
This one, please	To, proszę	*to prosheh*
That's fine	Dobrze	*dobzhe*
Nothing else, thank you	To wszystko, dziękuję	*to fshistko djenkooyeh*
I'll take it	Biorę	*byoreh*
I'll think about it	Pomyślę o tym	*pomishleh o tym*
Do you have a bag, please?	Czy mogę dostać torbę?	*chi mogeh dostach torbeh*
Can you wrap it, please?	Czy może pan/pani to zawinąć?	*chi mozhe pan/ panee to zaveenonch*
It's a gift	To prezent	*to prezent*
Where do I pay?	Gdzie mogę zapłacić?	*gdje mogeh zapwacheech*
Do you take credit cards?	Czy przyjmujecie karty kredytowe?	*chi pshiymooyeche karti kreditove*
I'm sorry I don't have any change	Przepraszam, nie mam drobnych	*psheprasham nye mam drobnih*
Can you give me a receipt, please?	Czy mogę dostać rachunek?	*chi mogeh dostach kfeet rahoonek*

Buying food and drink

A kilo of grapes, please	Kilo winogron, proszę	*keelo veenogron prosheh*
Half a kilo of tomatoes	Pół kilo pomidorów, proszę	*poow keelo pomeedoroof prosheh*
Two hundred grams of sweets	Dwieście gramów cukierków	*dvyeshche gramoof tsookyerkoof*
A piece of sausage, please	Kawałek kiełbasy, proszę	*kavawek kyewbasi prosheh*
Sliced	Pokrojone	*pokroyone*
A piece of cheese, please	Kawałek sera, proszę	*kavawek sera prosheh*
Five slices of ham, please	Pięć plasterków szynki, proszę	*pyench plasterkoof shinkee prosheh*
A bottle of red wine, please	Butelkę czerwonego wina, proszę	*bootelkeh chervonego veena prosheh*
A litre of water, please (fizzy/still)	Litr wody, proszę (z gazem/bez gazu)	*leetr vodi prosheh (z gazem/bez gazoor*
Half a litre of milk, please	Pół litra mleka, proszę	*poow leetra mleka prosheh*
Two cans of beer, please	Dwie puszki piwa, proszę	*dvye pooshkee peeva prosheh*
A bit of that, please	Kawałek tego, proszę	*kavawek tego prosheh*
A bit more/less	Trochę więcej/mniej	*troheh vyentsey/mney*
What is this?	Co to jest?	*tso to yest*

At the chemist

(see also Health, page 90)

Aspirins, please	Proszę aspirynę	*prosheh aspeerineh*
Plasters, please	Proszę plaster	*prosheh plaster*
Do you have something for diarrhoea?	Czy jest coś na rozwolnienie?	*chi yest tsosh na rozvolnyenye*
Do you have something for headaches?	Czy jest coś na ból głowy?	*chi yest tsosh na bool gwovi*

Buying clothes and shoes

I'm looking for a dress/shirt	Chcę suknię/koszulę	*htseh sooknyeh/ koshooleh*
I want some sandals	Chcę sandałki	*htse sandawkee*
I'm size 40	Mój rozmiar jest czterdzieści	*mooy rozmyar yest chterdjeshchee*
Can I try it on?	Czy mogę przymierzyć?	*chi mogeh pshimyezhich*
I like it	Podoba mi się	*podoba mee sheh*
I don't like it	Nie podoba mi się	*nye podoba mee sheh*
Do you have it in other colours?	Czy można to dostać w) innym kolorze?	*chi mozhna to dostach v eennim kolozhe*
It's too big/small	Za duże/małe	*za doozhe/mawe*
Have you got a smaller/ bigger size?	Czy jest mniejszy/ większy rozmiar?	*chi yest mnyeyshi/ vyenkshi rozmyar*

Miscellaneous

Five stamps for England, please	Pięć znaczków do Anglii, proszę	*pyench znachkoof do anglee prosheh*
Three postcards, please	Trzy karty, proszę	*tshi karty prosheh*
A box of matches, please	Pudełko zapałek, proszę	*poodewko zapawek prosheh*
A film for this camera, please	Film do tego aparatu, proszę	*feelm do tego aparatoo prosheh*
Do you have any English newspapers?	Czy są jakieś angielskie gazety?	*chi so yakyesh angyelskye gazeti*

You may hear

Kto następny?	*kto nastempni*	Who's next?
Słucham?	*swooham*	Can I help you?
Jaki rozmiar?	*yakee rozmyar*	What size?
Może być?	*mozhe bich*	Is that all right?

Sightseeing

▮ You can get information about all the sights worth seeing from **Polorbis Travel Ltd.** (address, page 134) and from local tourist information offices. The latter can tell you about attractive parts of Poland, organized trips, transportation services, cultural and sports events etc.

You may see

Godziny otwarcia/zwiedzania	Opening/visiting hours
Kasa	Ticket office
Nieczynne	Closed
Nie deptać trawników	Keep off the grass
Nie dotykać	Do not touch
Otwarte	Open
Prywatne	Private
Wstęp tylko dla upoważnionych	No entry
Wycieczki z przewodnikiem	Guided tours

You may want to say

(see also At the tourist office, page 49 for asking for information, brochures, etc.)

Opening times

(see Time, page 122)

When is the museum open?	**Kiedy museum jest otwarte?**	*kyedi moozeoom yest otfarte*

| What time does the palace close? | O której zamyka się pałac? | o ktoorey zamika sheh pawats |
| Is it open on Sundays? | Czy jest otwarte w niedzielę? | chi yest otfarte v nyedjeleh |

Visiting places

One/two, please	Jeden/dwa, proszę	yeden/dva prosheh
Two adults and a child	Dwa dla dorosłych i dziecko	dva dla doroswih ee djetsko
Is there a reduction for children?	Czy jest zniżka dla dzieci?	chi yest zneeshka dla djechee
For students	Dla studentów	dla stoodentoof
For pensioners	Dla emerytów	dla emeritoof
For the disabled	Dla inwalidów	dla invaleedoof
For groups	Grupowe	groopove
Are there guided tours?	Czy są wycieczki z przewodnikiem?	chi so vichechkee s pshevodneekyem
Can I/we take photos?	Czy można robić zdjęcia?	chi mozhna robeech zdyencha
When was this built?	Kiedy było to zbudowane?	kyedi biwo to zboodovane
Who painted that picture?	Kto namalował ten obraz?	kto namalovaw ten obras
When?	Kiedy?	kyedi
What time is mass?	O której jest msza?	o ktoorey yest msha

Sightseeing excursions

Are there any trips to Kazimierz?	Czy są wycieczki do Kazimierza?	chi so vichechkee do kazheemyezha
What time do I/we have to be here?	O której trzeba być?	o ktoorey tsheba bich
What time do we get back?	O której wracamy?	o ktoorey vratsami

Does the guide speak English?	**Czy przewodnik mówi po angielsku?**	*chi pshevodneek moovee po angyelskoo*
How much is it?	**Ile to kosztuje?**	*eele to koshtooye*

You may hear

Muzeum jest otwarte codziennie z wyjątkiem poniedziałków	*moozeoom yest otfarte tsodjennye z viyontkyem ponyedjawkoof*	The museum is open every day except Monday
Zamek został zbudowany w piętnastym wieku	*zamek zostaw zboodovani f pyetnastim vyekoo*	The castle was built in the fifteenth century
Ten obraz namalował Matejko	*ten obras namalovaw mateyko*	This picture was painted by Matejko
Autokar odjeżdża o godzinie dziesiątej z placu Konstytucji	*awtokar odyezhdja o godjeenye djeshontey s platsoo konstittootsee*	The coach leaves at ten o'clock from Konstytucji Square

Sports and activities

❚ Among the outdoor activities you can pursue in Poland are: mountaineering, hiking, horse riding, hunting, fishing, sailing and canoeing, not to mention sunbathing on the beaches – the weather in summer is often warm and sunny. When the white flag is flying on the beach, it is safe to bathe, when the red flag is flying you should bathe with caution and when the flag is black, bathing is prohibited.

❚ The mountain areas in the south of Poland offer plenty of opportunities for winter sports, particularly skiing and cross-country skiing. Ski trails are marked in four different colours according to difficulty: black, red, blue and green for competition-level, advanced, intermediate and beginner slopes.

❚ For riding enthusiasts, there are numerous equestrian centres. Vacations in the saddle – **wakacje w siodle** – are a very popular form of holiday in Poland.

❚ If you are interested in hunting, you will need to make arrangements in advance through a travel agency collaborating with '**Łowex**', or '**Animex**', or through an **Orbis** representative.

❚ It is also possible to 'take the waters' at a Polish spa centre – **uzdrowisko**. There are about fifty of them, often located in scenic areas, offering natural water treatment.

You may see

Basen (odkryty/zakryty)	Swimming pool (outdoor/indoor)
Kąpiel wzbroniona	No bathing
Kolejka górska	Cable car
Korty tenisowe	Tennis courts
Łowienie ryb wzbronione	No fishing
Niebezpieczeństwo (lawin)	Danger (of avalanches)

Plaża	Beach
Pływalnia	Swimming pool
Szkoła narciarska	Ski school
Teren łowiecki	Hunting grounds
Tor wyścigowy	Racetrack
Wyciąg krzesełkowy	Chairlift
Wyciąg narciarski	Ski lift
Wypożyczalnia sprzętu narciarskiego	Ski hire
Wypożyczalnia sprzętu wodnego	Water sports equipment hire
Wyścigi konne	Horse racing

You may want to say

General phrases

Can I/we hire bikes?	Czy można wypożyczyć rowery?	chi mozhna vipozhichich roveri
Can I/we go fishing?	Czy można łowić ryby?	chi mozhna woveech ryby
Can I/we go horse riding?	Czy można jeździć konno?	chi mozhna yezhdjeech konno
Where can we play tennis?	Gdzie można grać w tenisa?	gdje mozhna grach f teneesa
Where can I/we go climbing?	Gdzie można zrobić wycieczkę górską?	gdje mozhna zrobeech vichechkeh goorsko
I don't know how to ...	Nie umiem ... Nie umiem jeździć na nartach	nye oomyem nye oomyem yezhdjeech na nartah
I can ... a bit	Umiem trochę	oomyem troheh
Do you give lessons?	Czy dajecie lekcje?	chi dayeche lektsye
I'm a beginner	Jestem początkujący (male) /początkująca (female)	yestem pochontkooyontsy/ pochontkooyontsa

How much is it per hour?	Ile kosztuje za godzinę?	*eele koshtooye za godjeeneh*
How much is it for the whole day?	Ile kosztuje na cały dzień?	*eele koshtooye na tsawi djen*
Is there a reduction for children?	Czy jest zniżka dla dzieci?	*chi yest zneeshka dla djechee*
Can I/we hire equipment?	Czy można wypożyczyć sprzęt?	*chi mozhna vipozhichich spshent*
Can I/we hire rackets?	Czy można wypożyczyć rakietki?	*chi mozhna vipozhichich rakyetkee*
Is it necessary to be a member?	Czy trzeba być członkiem?	*chi tsheba bich chwonkyem*

Water sports

Can I/we swim here?	Czy można tu pływać?	*chi mozhna too pwivach*
Can I/we swim in the river?	Czy można pływać w rzece?	*chi mozhna pwivach v zhetse*
Is it dangerous?	Czy jest niebezpiecznie?	*chi yest nyebespyechnye*

Skiing

What is the snow like?	Jaki jest śnieg?	*yakee yest shnyek*
Is there a ski run for beginners?	Czy jest szlak narciarski dla początkujących?	*chi yest shlak narchyarskee dla pochontkooyontsih*
How much is the lift pass?	Ile kosztuje wyciąg?	*eele koshtooye vichonk*
Per day	Na dzień	*na djen*
Per week	Na tydzień	*na tidjen*
What time is the last ascent?	O której jest ostatni wyciąg?	*o ktoorey yest ostatnee vichonk*

Czy pan/pani jest początkujący (male) / **początkująca** (female)?	*chi pan/**panee** yest pochontkoo**yon**tsi/ pochontkoo**yon**tsa*	Are you a beginner?
Czy umie pan/pani żeglować?/jeździć konno?	*chi **oo**mye pan/**panee** zhe**glo**vach/ **yezh**djeech **kon**no*	Do you know how to sail?/ride a horse?
Proszę przyjść później	*pro*sheh pshiyshch **poozh**nyey*	Please come back later

Medical details - to show to a doctor

(Tick boxes or fill in details)

		Self a	Other members of family/party
Blood group	**Grupa krwi**		
Asthmatic	**Astmatyk**		
Blind	**Niewidomy**		
Deaf	**Głuchy**		
Diabetic	**Cukrzyk**		
Epileptic	**Epileptyk**		
Handicapped	**Upośledzony**		
Heart condition	**Chory na serce**		
High blood pressure	**Wysokie ciśnienie krwi**		
Pregnant	**Ciężarna**		
Allergic to ...	**Uczulony na ...**		
Antibiotics	**Antybiotyki**		
Penicillin	**Penicylina**		
Cortisone	**Kortyzon**		
Medicines	**Leki**		
For myself	**Dla mnie**		
For him/her	**Dla niego/niej**		

You can consult a doctor at a regional out-patient clinic – **przychodnia rejonowa** – or at a hospital – **szpital**. In addition, there are medical co-operatives – **spółdzielnia lekarska** – or you can go direct to a specialist private doctor.

If you need an ambulance – **pogotowie** – call either the police or the ambulance number. (See Emergencies, page 189).

At a chemist – **Apteka** – you can often get medical advice and first aid, as well as obtain certain medicines without a doctor's prescription.

To indicate where the pain is, you can simply point and say 'it hurts here' (**tu boli**). Otherwise, you'll need to look up the Polish for the appropriate part of the body (see page 94).

Notice that in Polish you refer to 'the head', 'the stomach', (**głowa**, **brzuch**), etc. rather than 'my head', 'my stomach'.

You may see

Apteka	Chemist
Do użycia zewnętrznego	For external use only
Klinika	Clinic
Lekarz	Doctor
Pogotowie	Ambulance
Potrząsnąć przed użyciem	Shake before using
Przychodnia rejonowa	Out-patients (regional)
Punkt pierwszej pomocy	First aid post
Sposób użycia	Instructions for use
Spółdzielnia lekarska	Medical co-operative
Szpital	Hospital
Trucizna!	Poison!

You may want to say

At the surgery

I need a doctor	**Potrzebuję doktora**	*potshebooyeh doktora*
Quickly	**Szybko**	*shipko*

Is there someone who speaks English?	**Czy mówi ktoś po angielsku?**	*chi moovee ktosh po angyelskoo*
Can I make an appointment?	**Czy mogę zamówić wizytę?**	*chi mogeh zamooveech veeziteh*
It's my husband	**To mój mąż**	*to mooy monsh*
It's my wife	**To mója żona**	*to moya zhona*
It's my friend	**To mój znajomy** (male)/ **to moja znajoma** (female)	*to mooy znayomi/to moya znayoma*
It's my son	**To mój syn**	*to mooy sin*
It's my daughter	**To moja córka**	*to moya tsoorka*
How much will it cost?	**Ile to będzie kosztować?**	*eele to bendje koshtovach*

Your symptoms

I feel unwell	**Źle się czuję**	*zhle sheh chooyeh*
It hurts here	**Tu boli**	*too bolee*
My ... hurts (sg.)	**Boli mnie ...**	*bolee mnye*
My ... hurt (pl.)	**Bolą mnie ...**	*bolo mnye*
My eyes hurt	**Bolą mnie oczy**	*bolo mnye ochee*
My feet hurt	**Bolą mnie stopy**	*bolo mnye stopi*
My stomach hurts	**Boli mnie brzuch**	*bolee mnye bzhooh*
My back hurts	**Bolą mnie plecy**	*bolo mnye pletsi*
I have a sore throat	**Boli mnie gardło**	*bolee mnye gardwo*
I have a temperature	**Mam gorączkę**	*mam goronchkeh*
I have diarrhoea	**Mam rozwolnienie**	*mam rozvolnyenye*
I feel dizzy/sick	**Niedobrze mi**	*nyedobzhe mee*
I have been sick	**Wymiotowałem** (male)/ **wymiotowałam** (female)	*vimyotovawem/ vimyotovawam*
I can't sleep	**Nie mogę spać**	*nye mogeh spach*
I can't breathe	**Nie mogę oddychać**	*nye mogeh oddihach*
I can't move my ...	**Nie mogę poruszyć ...**	*nye mogeh porooshich*
I'm bleeding	**Mam krwotok**	*mam krfotok*
It's my arm	**Moja ręka**	*moya renka*

It's my wrist	Moja kostka	*moya kostka*
I think that ...	To chyba ...	*to hiba*
It's broken	Jest złamane	*yest zwamane*
It's sprained	Jest zwichnięte	*yest zveehnyente*
I have cut myself	Przeciąłem się (male)/ przecięłam się (female)	*pshechowem sheh/ pshechewam sheh*
I have burnt myself	Oparzyłem się (male)/ oparzyłam się (female)	*opazhiwem sheh/ opazhiwam sheh*
I have been stung by an insect	Użądlił mnie owad	*oozhondleew mnye ovat*
I have been bitten by a dog	Ugryzł mnie pies	*oogris mnye pyes*

Someone else's symptoms

He/she feels unwell	On/ona źle się czuje	*on/ona zhle sheh chooye*
He/she is unconscious	On jest nieprzytomny (male)/ona jest nieprzytomna (female)	*on yest nyepshitomny/ ona yest nyepshitomna*
It hurts here	Tu boli	*too bolee*
His/her... hurt(s)	Boli go /ją...	*bolee go/yo*
His/her stomach hurts	Boli go /ją brzuch	*bolee go/yo bzhooh*
His/her back hurts	Bolą go/ją plecy	*bolą go/yo pletsi*
His/her eyes hurt	Bolą go/ją oczy	*bolo go/yo ochi*
His/her feet hurt	Bolą go/ją stopy	*bolo go/yo stopi*
He/she has a sore throat	Boli go/ją gardło	*bolee go/yo gardwo*
He/she has a temperature	On/ona ma gorączkę	*on/ona ma goronchkeh*
He/she has diarrhoea	On/ona ma rozwolnienie	*on/ona ma rozvolnyenye*
He/she feels dizzy/sick	Jemu/jej jest niedobrze	*yemoo/yey yest nyedobzhe*
He/she has been sick	Zwymiotował (male) zwymiotowała (female)	*zvimyotovaw/ zvimyotovawa*
He/she is bleeding	On/ona ma krwotok	*on/ona ma krfotok*

It's his/her ...	**To jego/jej ...**	*to yego/yey*
It's his/her ankle	**To jego/jej kostka**	*to yego/yey kostka*
It's his/her leg	**To jego/jej noga**	*to yego/yey noga*
He has cut himself /she has cut herself	**On przeciął się/ona przecięła się**	*on pshechow sheh /ona pshechewa sheh*
He has burnt himself /she has burnt herself	**On oparzył się/ona oparzyła się**	*on opazhiw sheh /ona opazhiwa sheh*
He/she has been stung by an insect	**Użądlił go** (him)/**ją** (her) **owad**	*oozhondleew go/yo ovat*
He/she has been bitten by a dog	**Ugryzł go** (him)/**ją** (her) **pies**	*oogris go/yo pyes*

You may hear

Co się stało?	*tso sheh stawo*	What happened?
Gdzie boli?	*gdje bolee*	Where does it hurt?
Proszę się rozebrać	*proshe sheh rozebrach*	Please get undressed
To nic groźnego	*to neets grozhnego*	It's nothing serious

Parts of the body

ankle	**kostka u nogi**	*kostka oo nogee*
appendix	**wyrostek**	*virostek*
arm	**ramię**	*ramyeh*
back	**plecy**	*pletsi*
bladder	**pęcherz**	*penhesh*
blood	**krew**	*kref*
body	**ciało**	*chawo*
bone	**kość**	*koshch*
bottom	**siedzenie**	*shedzenye*
bowels	**jelita**	*yeleeta*
breast	**pierś**	*pyersh*

buttock	pośladek	*poshladek*
cartilage	chrząstka	*hshonstka*
chest	klatka piersiowa	*klatka pyershova*
chin	podbródek	*podbroodek*
ear	ucho	*ooho*
face	twarz	*tfash*
finger	palec	*palets*
foot	stopa	*stopa*
genitals	genitalia	*geneetalya*
gland	gruczoł	*groochow*
hair	włosy	*vlosi*
hand	ręka	*renka*
head	głowa	*gwova*
heart	serce	*sertse*
heel	pięta	*pyenta*
hip	biodro	*byodro*
jaw	szczęka	*shchenka*
joint	staw	*staf*
kidney	nerka	*nerka*
knee	kolano	*kolano*
leg	noga	*noga*
ligament	wiązadło	*vionzadwo*
lip	warga	*varga*
liver	wątroba	*vontroba*
lung	płuco	*pwootso*
mouth	usta	*oosta*
muscle	mięsleń	*myenshen*
nail	paznokieć	*paznokyech*
neck	szyja	*shiya*
nerve	nerw	*nerv*
nose	nos	*nos*

penis	członek	*chwonek*
rectum	odbytnica	*odbytneetsa*
rib	żebro	*zhebro*
shoulder	ramię	*ramyeh*
skin	skóra	*skoora*
spine	kręgosłup	*krengoswoop*
stomach	brzuch or żołądek	*bzhooh/zhowondek*
tendon	ścięgno	*shchengno*
testicles	jądra	*yondra*
thigh	udo	*oodo*
throat	gardło	*gardwo*
thumb	kciuk	*kchook*
toe	palec u nogi	*palets oo nogee*
tongue	język	*yenzik*
tonsils	migdałki	*meegdawkee*
tooth	ząb	*zomp*
vagina	pochwa	*pohfa*
wrist	kostka u ręki	*kostka oo renkee*

Problems and complaints

(For car breakdowns, see Road Travel, page 24; see also Emergencies, page 188)

▌ There are four types of police in Poland, all of them armed. They are:

▌ **Policja Porządkowa** (municipal police) – the regular police force, responsible for law and order in the streets. They wear dark grey-blue uniforms.

▌ **Policja Drogowa** (road traffic police). They wear navy-blue uniforms with white hats and orange arm reflectors.

▌ **Straż Miejska** (city guard), who wear dark-blue uniforms. They correspond roughly to traffic wardens in Britain, but they are also present when there are demonstrations and strikes.

▌ **Policja Kryminalna** (criminal police). They also wear dark grey-blue uniforms, and are responsible for crime in general.

▌ There is also **Oddziały Specjalne** – a 'special branch' section of the police force, dealing with terrorist crime and high-level corruption.

▌ If you lose your passport or have something stolen, contact your hotel management; they will put you in touch with the police, and/or the British/American Consulate, or you can go direct to the municipal or criminal police.

▌ In a hotel, if all else fails and you can't get a complaint sorted out to your satisfaction, you can ask for the complaints book – **Książka życzeń i zażaleń**.

You may see

Książka życzeń i zażaleń   Complaints book

Nagły wypadek	Emergency
Nie działa	Out of order
Nieczynne	Out of order or closed
Posterunek policji	Police station
Straż pożarna	Fire brigade

You may want to say

General phrases

I need help	**Potrzebuję pomocy**	potshebooyeh pomotsi
Can you fix it (immediately)?	**Czy można to (zaraz) naprawić?**	chi mozhna to zaras napraveech
When can you fix it?	**Kiedy to może być naprawione?**	kyedi to mozhe bich napravyone
Can I speak to the manager?	**Czy mogę rozmawiać z kierownikiem?**	chi mogeh rozmavyach s kyerovneekyem
Here is the problem ...	**Tu jest problem ...**	too yest problem
There isn't/aren't any ...	**Nie ma ...**	nye ma
I need ...	**Potrzebuję ...**	potshebooyeh
It doesn't work	**Nie działa**	nye djawa
It's broken	**Jest złamane**	yest zwamane
It's missing	**Brakuje ...**	brakooye
I can't ...	**Nie mogę ...**	nye mogeh
It wasn't my fault	**To nie moja wina**	to nye moya veena
I've forgotten my ...	**Zapomniałem** (male)/ **zapomniałam** (female) ...	zapomnyawem/ zapomnyawam...
I've lost my ...	**Zgubiłem** (male) **zgubiłam** (female)...	zgoobeewem/ zgoobeewam
We've lost our ...	**Zgubiliśmy ...**	zgoobeeleeshmi
Someone has stolen my ...	**Ukradziono mi mój ...**	ookradjono mee mooy

It has disappeared	**Zniknęło**	*zneeknewo*
Something is missing	**Brakuje czegoś**	*brakooye chegosh*
This isn't mine	**To nie moje**	*to nye moye*

Where you're staying

There isn't any hot water	**Nie ma ciepłej wody**	*nye ma chepwey vodi*
There isn't any toilet paper	**Nie ma papieru toaletowego**	*nye ma papyeroo toaletovego*
There isn't any electricity	**Nie ma prądu**	*nye ma prondoo*
There aren't any towels	**Nie ma ręczników**	*nye ma renchneekoof*
Another blanket, please	**Jeszcze jeden koc proszę**	*yeshche yeden kots prosheh*
I need a light bulb	**Potrzebna żarówka**	*potshebna zharoofka*
The light doesn't work	**Światło nie działa**	*shfyatwo nye djawa*
The shower doesn't work	**Prysznic nie działa**	*prishneets nye djawa*
The lock is broken	**Zamek jest zepsuty**	*zamek yest zepsooti*
The switch on the lamp is broken	**Lampa nie działa**	*lampa nye djawa*
I can't open the window	**Nie mogę otworzyć okna**	*nye mogeh otfozhich okna*
The toilet doesn't flush	**Nie można spuścić wody w ubikacji**	*nye mozhna spooshcheech vodi v oobeekatsee*
The washbasin is blocked	**Umywalka zapchała się**	*oomivalka zaphawa sheh*
The washbasin is dirty	**Umywalka jest brudna**	*oomivalka yest broodna*
It's very noisy	**Jest duży hałas**	*yest doozhi hawas*
There's a smell of gas	**Czuć gaz**	*chooch gas*

In bars and restaurants

This isn't cooked	**To jest surowe**	*to yest surove*
This is burnt	**To jest spalone**	*to yest spalone*

This is cold	To jest zimne	to yest *zheem*ne
I didn't order this, I ordered ...	Nie zamówiłem (male) nie zamówiłam (female) tego, zamówiłem/ zamówiłam ...	*nye zamooveewem/ nye zamooveewam tego, zamooveewem/ zamooveewam*
This is dirty	To jest brudne	to yest *brood*ne
This smells bad	To śmierdzi	to *shmyer*djee
There is a mistake on the bill	Jest pomyłka w rachunku	yest pomiwka v ra*hoon*koo

In shops

I bought this here (yesterday)	Kupiłem (male)/kupiłam (female) to tutaj (wczoraj)	koo*pee*wem/ koo*pee*wam to *too*tay *(fcho*ray)
Can I change this?	Czy mogę to zamienić?	chi *mo*geh to zam*ye*neech
I want to return this	Zwracam to	*zvrat*sam to
Can I have a refund?	Czy dostanę zwrot pieniędzy?	chi do*sta*neh zvrot pye*nyen*dzi
It has a flaw in it	Ma wadę	ma *va*deh
There is a stain	Jest plama	yest *pla*ma
This is off/rotten	To jest zepsute	to yest zep*soo*te

Forgetting and losing things; theft

I've forgotten my tickets	Zapomniałem (male)/ zapomniałam (female) biletu	zapom*nya*wem/ zapom*nya*wam bee*le*too
I've forgotten the key	Zapomniałem (male)/ zapomniałam (female) kluczy	zapom*nya*wem/ zapom*nya*wam *kloo*chi
I've lost my wallet	Zgubiłem (male / zgubiłam (female) portfel	zgoo*bee*wem/ zgoo*bee*wam *port*fel

I have lost my driving licence	**Zgubiłem** (male)/ **zgubiłam** (female) **prawo jazdy**	*zgoobeewem/ zgoobeewam* **pravo yaz**di
We have lost our rucksacks	**Zgubiliśmy nasze plecaki**	*zgoobee**leesh**mi nashe pletsakee*
Where is the lost property office?	**Gdzie jest biuro rzeczy znalezionych?**	*gdje yest **byoo**ro **zhe**chi znalezhonih*
Where is the police station?	**Gdzie jest posterunek policji?**	*gdje yest poster**oo**nek poleetsee*
Someone has stolen my bag	**Ukradziono mi torbę**	*ookrad**jo**no mee **tor**beh*
Someone has stolen the car	**Ukradziono mi samochód**	*ookrad**jo**no mee samo**hoot***
Someone has stolen my money	**Ukradziono mi pieniądze**	*ookrad**jo**no mee pye**nyon**dze*

If someone is bothering you

Please leave me alone	**Proszę dać mi spokój**	*prosheh dach mee **spo**kooy*
Go away or I'll call the police	**Proszę się odczepić albo zawołam policję**	*prosheh sheh ot**che**peech albo zavowam **pol**eetsyeh*
There is someone bothering me	**Ktoś naprzykrza mi się**	*ktosh na**pshik**sha mee sheh*
There is someone following me	**Ktoś idzie za mną**	*ktosh **ee**dje za mno*

You may hear

Helpful and unhelpful remarks

| **Proszę chwilę zaczekać** | *prosheh **hfee**le za**che**kach* | Wait a moment, please |
| **Proszę bardzo** | *prosheh **bar**dzo* | Here you are |

101

Niestety nic nie da się zrobić	*nyesteti neets nye da sheh zrobeech*	Unfortunately, nothing can be done
Nie wiem	*nye vyem*	I don't know

Questions you may be asked

Kiedy pan/pani to zgubił (male)/**zgubiła** (female)**?**	*kyedi pan/panee to zgoobeew/zgoobeewa*	When did you lose it?
Kiedy to się stało?	*kyedi to sheh stawo*	When did it happen?
Jak wygląda samochód?	*yak viglonda samohoot*	What does the car look like?
Proszę wypełnić ten formularz	*prosheh vipewneech ten formoolash*	Please fill in this form

Basic grammar

▌ Polish belongs to the Slavonic group of languages which includes Russian, Czech, Ukrainian, Serbo-Croat and a few other East European languages. The most typical feature of these languages is the case system, i.e. a complex system of word endings indicating different meanings. For example, 'I like rainy weather' is **'lubię deszczową pogodę'** whereas 'we don't like rainy weather' is **'nie lubimy deszczowej pogody'**; 'I (female) went to the cinema yesterday' is **'poszłam wczoraj do kina'**, whereas 'I (male) went to the cinema yesterday' is **'poszedłem wczoraj do kina'**. Thus, almost every word will have several different forms, usually expressed as different endings.

Nouns

All Polish nouns have a grammatical gender: masculine, feminine or neuter. Thus, **kobieta** (woman) is feminine, **chłopiec** (boy) is masculine, and **dziecko** (child) is neuter. However, in most cases the grammatical gender is not related to its meaning, and is determined only by the ending of the noun.

Most masculine nouns end in a consonant: **pies** (dog), **obraz** (painting), **rok** (year). Some exceptions are masculine nouns ending in -a: **kierowca** (driver), **mężczyzna** (man). A typical masculine surname ending is **-ski** or **-cki: Jacek Kowalski**.

Most nouns ending in -a are feminine: **książka** (book), **praca** (work), **opona** (tyre). Some feminine nouns end in a consonant: **solidarność** (solidarity), **miłość.** (love), **noc** (night). It's important to remember at this point that all feminine given names end in -a: **Katarzyna, Iwona**. The same goes for surnames ending in **-ska, -cka: Katarzyna Kowalska.**

Neuter nouns end in **-o**, **-e**, or **-ę**: **okno** (window), **morze** (sea), **imię** (first name).

Each noun may appear in any of the six cases listed below, depending on what is being expressed in a sentence. The complexity of the case system means that each noun can have as many as twelve different endings. The best thing is to try to recognize the main part of the word and not worry too much about the endings.

Nominative (the dictionary form) – the subject of the sentence; a person or thing performing the action, or in introductions following **to jest ...** (this is ...) e.g. **to jest mój syn** (this is my son).

Accusative – the direct object of the sentence: **odwiedzam mojego syna** (I'm visiting my son).

Genitive – to express possession: **żona mojego syna** (my son's wife); after negation: **nie ma mojego syna** (my son isn't here); after adverbs of quantity: **kilku moich synów** (several of my sons); after some prepositions: **jadę do mojego syna** (I'm going to my son's).

Dative – the indirect object, a person or a thing to whom something happens: **dałam present mojemu synowi** (I gave a present to my son).

Instrumental – points to the instrument with which something is done; doing something together: **mieszkam razem z moim synem** (I live together with my son).

Locative (prepositional) – used only after certain prepositions: **rozmawiamy o moim synu** (we're talking about my son).

In addition, all nouns are divided into animate (living things, e.g. dog) or inanimate (non-living things e.g. table) which in turn affects their declension.

Plurals

Plurals of nouns are formed in a variety of ways, depending on the gender and the last letter of the noun. Again, it's best not to worry too much about the plural, at least to begin with.

Articles ('a' and 'the')

In one way at least, Polish is simpler than English in that it doesn't use articles in front of nouns. If you want to say 'what a lovely day' in Polish it is: **jaki piękny dzień**. 'In the evening' is simply **wieczorem.**

Demonstrative pronouns ('this', 'that', 'these', 'those')

Singular

Ten – (masculine): **ten dom** (this house)

Ta – (feminine): **ta dziewczynka** (this girl)

To – (neuter): **to dziecko** (this child)

Like nouns, they have different forms in different cases:

daj present temu dziecku/tej dziewczynce (give a present to this child/this girl; Dative).

Plural

Ci – (masculine, human only): **ci chłopcy** (these boys)

Te – (all others): **te dziewczyny, te koty** (these girls, these cats)

They appear in different forms in different cases, e.g.: **nie widzę tych kotów** (I can't see these cats; Genitive).

Personal pronouns
('I', 'you', 'he', 'she', etc.)

Notice two forms for 'they' in Polish: **oni** (masc. and mixed gender) and **one** (women, feminine objects, animals and things).

Singular (Nominative)		Plural (Nominative)	
I	**ja**	we	**my**
you	**ty**	you	**wy**
he	**on**		
she	**ona**	they	**oni, one**
it	**ono**		

They have different forms in different cases, e.g.:

ona chce się ze mną bawić (she wants to play with me)

on jest z nimi (he is with them)

napisz do niej (write to her).

Possessives ('my', 'his', 'her', etc.)

Singular (Nominative)		Plural (Nominative)	
my	**mój, moja, moje**	our	**nasz, nasza, nasze**
your	**twój, twoja, twoje**	your	**wasz, wasza, wasze**
his, her, its	**jego, jej**	their	**ich**

They have different forms in different cases, e.g.:

nie widzę naszych dzieci (I can't see our children)

There is no Polish equivalent to the English apostrophe **'s** as in 'John's brother'; this is expressed by the Genitive ending instead: **dom mojego ojca** (my father's house).

Adjectives

Adjectives agree in number and gender with the nouns they are describing. They have the following endings in the Nominative case: **-i**, **-y** in masculine; **-a** in feminine, and **-e** in neuter and plural, e.g.:

biały dom	(white house)
tani samochód	(cheap car)
ładna pogoda	(nice weather)
spokojne morze	(calm sea)

In the nominative plural the ending is **-e** for all genders: **białe domy**, **tanie samochody**.

Here are examples of how they change:

Ładna pogoda	(nice weather)
Jaka ładna pogoda!	What lovely weather! (Nominative)
Nie ma ładnej pogody	The weather isn't good (Genitive)
Przy ładnej pogodzie	When the weather is nice (Locative)
Tani samochód	(cheap car)
Nie kupię taniego samochodu	I won't buy a cheap car (Genitive)
Jeżdżę tanim samochodem	I drive a cheap car (Instrumental)
Wolę tanie samochody	I prefer cheap cars (Accusative plural)
Nie sprzedajemy tanich samochodów	We don't sell cheap cars (Genitive plural)

Most adjectives come before the noun, as in the examples above.

Surnames ending in **-ski**, **-cki** (masculine) and **-ska**, **-cka** (feminine) have adjectival endings, e.g.:

Dyrektora Kowalskiego nie ma w biurze (Mr Kowalski, the director, isn't in the office);

Jestem umówiony z panią Białecką (I've got an appointment with Mrs Białecka).

Comparatives and superlatives
('more', 'the most')

Most adjectives form comparatives by adding **-ejszy** or **-szy**, and the superlative by adding the prefix **naj-** :

ładny – ładniejszy – najładniejszy (lovely, lovelier, the loveliest);

tani – tańszy – najtańszy (cheap, cheaper, the cheapest).

Some, particularly the longer ones, put the word **bardziej** and **najbardziej** at the front:

elegancki – bardziej elegancki – najbardziej elegancki (elegant, more elegant, the most elegant).

Some adjectives are irregular and their comparatives are completely different:

zły – gorszy – najgorszy (bad, worse, the worst);

dobry – lepszy – najlepszy (good, better, the best).

There is also a group of adjectives ending in **-ski** or **-cki** (masculine); **-ska, -cka** (feminine); **-skie, -ckie** (neuter and plural) which are worth remembering, since many typical Polish surnames end with them, e.g.: **Kowalski**, **Laskowska**; also, the names of languages have the masculine ending: **włoski, francuski, niemiecki** (Italian, French, German).

Ordinals

(See Numbers, page 114)

Ordinals, like adjectives, agree with the nouns, and follow the same declension as other words describing nouns: **pierwszy, drugi, trzeci**, etc.

Other words belonging to the group describing the noun and behaving like adjectives are: Question words: **który? jaki? czyj?**

to?, co? (which, whose, who, what); the -ing forms: **piszący, dący** (writing, travelling, as in 'a writing/travelling person').

Verbs

Tenses – perfect and imperfect

A typical feature of Polish verbs is that almost all of them have two different forms in the infinitive and in the past and future tense forms, depending on whether one is expressing the completeness of the action – perfect verbs, or the incompleteness of the action – imperfect verbs. The English language uses the continuous forms of the verb in the latter case, e.g.: 'I was reading a book', whereas in Polish you would use the imperfect form of the verb **czytać**: **czytałam książkę** (masculine), or **czytałem książkę** (feminine). The corresponding perfect form is **przeczytałem/przeczytałam książkę** (I read the book), meaning 'finished it'. There are several different ways in which verbs create their perfect forms; sometimes this form is totally unrelated, e.g.: **brać – wziąć** (take). The dictionary at the end of this book gives you the imperfect forms only, unless the verb has a completely different form, in which case both forms are given, e.g.: **brać – wziąć** (to take).

Because of the perfect/imperfect division of verbs, the language form encountered in written or spoken Polish is often quite different from the dictionary form of the verb.

Verbs have different endings according to person, number (singular or plural), tense (present, past and future) and gender (in the past tense only). For this reason, in this book the two forms – masculine and feminine – are given where necessary, e.g.: **chciałbym** (I would like; masculine) and **chciałabym** (feminine). Again, since it is impossible to master all these endings in a short time, the main thing is to try to recognise the basic element of the verb, rather than concentrating on the ending.

Here is an example of the verb 'to be': **być**.

Present tense

Singular		Plural	
I am	**ja jestem**	we are	**my jesteśmy**
you are	**ty jesteś**	you are	**wy jesteście**
he, she, it is	**on, ona, ono jest**	they are	**oni/one są**

Past tense

(Notice the distinction between 'men only' and 'women and things')

Singular		Plural	
I was	**ja byłem/byłam**	we were	**my byliśmy /byłyście**
you were	**ty byłeś/byłaś**	you were	**wy byliście/ byłyście**
he, she, it was	**on był, ona była, ono było**	they were	**oni byli/one były**

Future tense

Singular		Plural	
I will be	**ja będę**	we will be	**my będziemy**
you will be	**ty będziesz**	you will be	**wy będziecie**
he, she, it will be	**on, ona, ono będzie**	they will be	**oni, one będą**

Polish has two different verbs for 'to go': **iść** (on foot) and **jechać** (go by transport). Here is the conjugation pattern of these verbs (in imperfect forms):

Present

Singular		Plural	
I'm going	**idę, jadę**	we're going	**idziemy, jedziemy**
you're going	**idziesz, jedziesz**	you're going	**idziecie, jedziecie**
he, she, it is going	**idzie, jedzie**	they're going	**idą, jadą**

Past

Singular		Plural	
I was going	**szedłem, szłam jechałem, jechałam**	we were going/ went	**szliśmy, szłyśmy, jechaliśmy, jechałyśmy**
you were going	**szedłeś, szłaś, jechałeś, jechałaś**	you were going	**szliście, szłyście, jechaliście, jechałyście**
he, she, it was going	**szedł, szła, szło, jechał, jechała, jechało**	they were going	**szli, szły, jechali, jechały**

Future

Singular		Plural	
I'll be going	**będę iść/jechać**	we'll be going	**będziemy iść/ jechać**
you'll be going	**będziesz iść/ jechać**	you'll be going	**będziecie iść/ jechać**
he, she, it will be going	**będzie iść/ jechać**	they'll be going	**oni/one będą iść/ jechać**

Note on tenses

Bearing in mind that most verbs have the imperfect and perfect forms, their future tense can be formed in two ways: one is with the verb 'to be' followed by the imperfect infinitive of the main verb, as in the example above (imperfect); the other is future perfect, for which you need the perfect form. Using the perfect forms of the verbs demonstrated above: **iść – pójść**; **jechać – pojechać**, the future perfect looks like this:

Future perfect

Singular	Plural		
I'll go	**pójdę, pojadę**	we'll go	**pójdziemy, pojedziemy**
you'll go	**pójdziesz, pojedziesz**	you'll go	**pójdziecie, pojedziecie**
he, she, it'll go	**pójdzie, pojedzie**	they'll go	**pójdą, pojadą**

As far as the forms of address are concerned (explained in General conversation), the formal **pan/pani** forms take 3rd person singular endings: **gdzie pan/pani mieszka?** (where do you live?).

In the plural form **państwo** you use the 3rd person plural ending of the verb: **gdzie państwo mieszkają?**

Note: Infinitives end in **-ć**, e.g.: **jechać** (to go), **pracować** (to work).

Reflexives

Most transitive verbs, i.e. those taking an object, are followed by **się** if the object is the same as the subject of the sentence. e.g.: **ubieram się** (I'm dressing myself); **myje się** (he/she washes himself/herself).

Word order; absence of subject

Since both nouns and verbs indicate person, tense and gender, precisely by their endings, word order in Polish is fairly flexible and the subject of a complex sentence can often be found at the end. Moreover, the subject may not even be overtly present; the verb ending, again, will show who or what is meant as the subject. In the sentence: **dał jej książkę** (he gave her the book) the ending of the verb **-ł** indicates 3rd person singular past tense masculine subject. Often it is the word which receives special emphasis that appears at the beginning of the sentence, e.g. you can say: **jej dał książkę**, emphasizing the fact that it is *her* to whom he gave the book.

For the same reason, there is no need to use pronouns in the same way as in English. You say: **pracuję w biurze** (I work in an office), rather than: **ja pracuję ...**, since the ending **-ę** already indicates, in the present tense, first person singular.

Adverbs

Adverbs are words which usually describe verbs. They have the ending **-o** or **-e** (**tanio** – cheaply; **dobrze** – well).They can appear anywhere in the sentence, e.g. in front of the verb: **często pisze** (he/she writes often).

If you want to say what language you speak you use the adverbial expression: **mówię po polsku, po angielsku, po niemiecku,** etc. (I speak Polish, English, German, etc.).

Negatives

Negatives are formed by putting the word **nie** in front of the verb, e.g.: **nie mam dzieci** (I don't have any children); **nie rozumiem** (I don't understand); **nie ma owoców** (there is no fruit).

Polish uses double (or more) negatives: **nigdy nic nie rozumiesz** (you never understand anything); here **nic** means 'nothing', **nigdy** 'never', **nie** 'not'.

Questions

The word order in questions is the same as in ordinary statement. To indicate that you are asking a question you make your voice rise at the end of the sentence.

Yes/no questions can be preceded by the question word **czy.** Although it's not necessary to use it, in this book yes/no questions are preceded by **czy,** since this is a good way to draw attention to yourself: **czy mogę tu zaparkować?** (can I park here?); **czy to jest główna ulica?** (is this the main street?).

Cardinals

0	zero	*zero*
1	jeden	*yeden*
2	dwa	*dva*
3	trzy	*tshi*
4	cztery	*chteri*
5	pięć	*pyench*
6	sześć	*sheshch*
7	siedem	*shedem*
8	osiem	*oshem*
9	dziewięć	*djevyench*
10	dziesięć	*djeshench*
11	jedenaście	*yedenashche*
12	dwanaście	*dvanashche*
13	trzynaście	*tshinashche*
14	czternaście	*chternashche*
15	piętnaście	*pyentnashche*
16	szesnaście	*shesnashche*
17	siedemnaście	*shedemnashche*
18	osiemnaście	*oshemnashche*
19	dziewiętnaście	*djevyentnashche*
20	dwadzieścia	*dvadjeshcha*
21	dwadzieścia jeden	*dvadjeshcha yeden*
22	dwadzieścia dwa	*dvadjeshcha dva*
23 etc.	dwadzieścia trzy itd.	*dvadjeshcha tshi*
30	trzydzieści	*tshidjeshchi*

1	trzydzieści jeden	*tshidjeshchi yeden*
2 etc.	trzydzieści dwa itd.	*tshidjeshchi dva*
0	czterdzieści	*chterdjeshchi*
0	pięćdziesiąt	*pyenchdjeshont*
0	sześćdziesiąt	*sheshchdjeshont*
0	siedemdziesiąt	*shedemdjeshont*
0	osiemdziesiąt	*oshemdjeshont*
0	dziewięćdziesiąt	*djevyenchdjeshont*
00	sto	*sto*
01 etc.	sto jeden itd.	*sto yeden*
00	dwieście	*dvyeshche*
00	trzysta	*tshista*
00	czterysta	*chterista*
00	pięćset	*pyenchset*
00	sześćset	*sheshchset*
00	siedemset	*shedemset*
00	osiemset	*oshemset*
00	dziewięćset	*djevyenchset*
,000	tysiąc	*tishonts*
,000 etc.	dwa tysiące	*dva tishontse*
,000 000	milion	*meelyon*
,000 000 etc.	dwa miliony itd.	*dva meelyoni*

Ordinals

Ordinals have adjectival endings and therefore agree with the nouns they describe in gender and number, e.g: 'first' in the Nominative case is **pierwszy** (masculine), **pierwsza** (feminine), **pierwsze** (neuter and plural). In the other cases it follows the adjectival declension (see Basic grammar, p 103).

Here is a list of ordinals in the masculine gender form:

1st	**pierwszy**	*pyerfshi*
2nd	**drugi**	*droogee*
3rd	**trzeci**	*tshechee*
4th	**czwarty**	*chfarti*
5th	**piąty**	*pyonti*
6th	**szósty**	*shoosti*
7th	**siódmy**	*shoodmi*
8th	**ósmy**	*oosmi*
9th	**dziewiąty**	*djevyonti*
10th	**dziesiąty**	*djeshonti*
11th	**jedenasty**	*yedenasti*
12th	**dwunasty**	*dvoonasti*
13th	**trzynasty**	*tshinasti*
14th	**czternasty**	*chternasti*
15th	**piętnasty**	*pyentnasti*
16th	**szesnasty**	*shesnasti*
17th	**siedemnasty**	*shedemnasti*
18th	**osiemnasty**	*oshemnasti*
19th	**dziewiętnasty**	*djevyentnasti*
20th	**dwudziesty**	*dvoodjesti*
21st etc.	**dwudziesty pierwszy itd.**	*dvoodjesti pyerfshi*
30th	**trzydziesty**	*tshidjesti*
40th	**czterdziesty**	*chterdjesti*
50th	**pięćdziesiąty**	*pyenchdjeshonti*
60th	**sześćdziesiąty**	*sheshchdjeshonti*
70th	**siedemdziesiąty**	*shedemdjeshonti*
80th	**osiemdziesiąty**	*oshemdjeshonti*
90th	**dziewięćdziesiąty**	*djevyenchdjeshonti*
100th	**setny**	*setni*
200th	**dwusetny**	*dvoosetni*

116

| 300th etc. | **trzysetny itd.** | *tshisetni* |
| 1000th | **tysięczny** | *tishenchni* |

Years:

The first two numbers are read as cardinals, the remaining two as ordinals:

| 1995 | tysiąc dziewięćset dziewięćdziesiąty piąty |
| 1457 | tysiąc czterysta pięćdziesiąty siódmy |

Days, months, dates

▌ Names of days and months are written with small letters.

Days

Monday	**poniedziałek**	*ponyedjawek*
Tuesday	**wtorek**	*ftorek*
Wednesday	**środa**	*shroda*
Thursday	**czwartek**	*chfartek*
Friday	**piątek**	*pyontek*
Saturday	**sobota**	*sobota*
Sunday	**niedziela**	*nyedjela*

Months

January	**styczeń**	*stichen*
February	**luty**	*looti*
March	**marzec**	*mazhets*
April	**kwiecień**	*kfyechen*
May	**maj**	*may*
June	**czerwiec**	*chervyets*
July	**lipiec**	*leepyets*
August	**sierpień**	*sherpyen*
September	**wrzesień**	*vzheshen*
October	**październik**	*pazhdjerneek*
November	**listopad**	*leestopat*
December	**grudzień**	*groodjen*

Seasons

spring	**wiosna**	*vyosna*
summer	**lato**	*lato*
autumn	**jesień**	*yeshen*
winter	**zima**	*zheema*

General phrases

day	**dzień**	*djen*
week	**tydzień**	*tidjen*
fortnight	**dwa tygodnie**	*dva tigodnye*
month	**miesiąc**	*myeshonts*
year	**rok**	*rok*

today	**dziś** or **dzisiaj**	*djeesh/djeeshay*
tomorrow	**jutro**	*yootro*
yesterday	**wczoraj**	*fchoray*

(in) the morning	**rano**	*rano*
(in) the afternoon/ evening	**po południu/ wieczorem**	*po powoodnyoo/ vyechorem*
(at) night	**w nocy**	*v notsi*
tomorrow morning	**jutro rano**	*yootro rano*
yesterday afternoon/ evening	**wczoraj po południu/ wieczorem**	*fchoray po powoodnyoo/ vyechorem*
last night	**wczoraj w nocy**	*fchoray v notsi*

on Monday	**w poniedziałek**	*f ponyedjawek*
on Tuesdays	**we wtorki**	*ve ftorkee*
every Wednesday	**w każdą środę**	*f kazhdo shrodeh*

119

in August	w sierpniu	f sherpnyoo
in spring	na wiosnę	na vyosneh
at the beginning of March	na początku marca	na pochontkoo martsa
in the middle of June	w środku czerwca	f shrotkoo cherftsa
at the end of September	w końcu września	f kontsoo vzheshnya

in six months' time	za sześć miesięcy	za sheshch myeshentsy
during the summer	latem	latem
two years ago	dwa lata temu	dva lata temoo
(in) the 1990s	w latach dziewięćdziesiątych	v latah djevyenchdjeshontih

last ...	w zeszły ...	v zeshwi ...
last Monday	w zeszły poniedziałek	v zeshwi ponyedjawek
last week	w zeszłym tygodniu	v zeshwim tigodnyoo
last month	w zeszłym miesiącu	v zeshwim myeshontsoo
last year	w zeszłym roku	v zeshwim rokoo

next ...	w przyszłym ...	f pshishwim/ nastempnim
next Tuesday	w przyszły wtorek	f pshishwi ftorek
next week	w przyszłym tygodniu	f pshishwim tigodnyoo
next month	w przyszłym miesiącu	f pshishwim myeshontsoo
next year	w przyszłym roku	f pshishwim rokoo

What day is it today?	Jaki dzisiaj dzień?	yakee djeeshay djen
What is the date today?	Którego dzisiaj jest?	ktoorego djeeshay yest
When is your birthday?	Kiedy są pana/pani urodziny?	kyedi so pana/ panee oorodjeeni
When is your saint's day (name day)?*	Kiedy są pana/pani imieniny?	kyedi so pana/panee eemyeneeni

120

It's (on) the first of January	**Pierwszego stycznia**	*pyerfshego stichnya*
(on) Tuesday 10th May	**We wtorek dziesiątego maja**	*ve ftorek dzieshontego maya*
1995	**Tysiąc dziewięćset dziewięćdziesiąty piąty**	*tishonts djevyenchset djevyendjeshonti pyonti*
The 15th century	**Piętnasty wiek**	*pyentnasti vyek*

* Poles celebrate the saint's day corresponding to their given name (name day – **imieniny**), rather than their birthday (**urodziny**).

Time

■ To tell the time in Polish, you need to know the ordinal numbers; (see Numbers, page 114).

Godzina in Polish means both 'o'clock' and 'hour'.

one o'clock	**pierwsza (godzina)**	*pyerfsha (godjeena)*
two o'clock	**druga**	*drooga*
four o'clock	**czwarta**	*chfarta*
six o'clock	**szósta**	*shoosta*
twelve o'clock	**dwunasta**	*dvoonasta*
a quarter past ...	**piętnaście po ...**	*pyentnashche po*
half past ...	**w pół do ...**	*f poow do*
five past ...	**pięć po ...**	*pyench po*
twenty-five past	**dwadzieścia pięć po ...**	*dvadjeshcha pyench po*
a quarter to ...	**za piętnaście** or **za kwadrans ...**	*za pyentnashche/za kfadrans*
ten to ...	**za dziesięć ...**	*za djeshench*
twenty to ...	**za dwadzieścia ...**	*za dvadjeshcha*
in the morning (a.m.)	**przed południem**	*pshet powoodnyem*
in the early morning	**rano**	*rano*
in the afternoon	**po południu**	*po powoodnyoo*
in the evening	**wieczorem**	*vyechorem*
at night	**w nocy**	*v notsi*
noon/midday	**południe**	*powoodnye*
midnight	**północ**	*poownots*
a quarter of an hour	**kwadrans**	*kfadrans*
three quarters of an hour	**trzy kwadranse**	*tshi kfadranse*
half an hour	**pół godziny**	*poow godjeeni*

24-hour clock

0000	**zero**	zero
0900	**dziewiąta (godzina)**	djevyonta (godjeena)
1300	**trzynasta**	tshinasta
1430	**czternasta trzydzieści**	chternasta tshidjeshchee
2149	**dwudziesta pierwsza**	dvoodjesta pyerfsha
	czterdzieści dziewięć	chterdjeshchee djevyench
at ...	**o ...**	o
exactly/precisely ...	**dokładnie o ...**	dokwadnye o
just after ...	**tuż po ...**	toosh po
about ...	**około ...**	okowo
approximately ...	**mniej więcej ...**	mnyey vyentsey
nearly ...	**prawie ...**	pravye
soon	**wkrótce**	fkrootse
early	**wcześnie**	fcheshnye
late	**późno**	poozhno
on time	**punktualnie**	poonktooalnye
earlier	**wcześniej**	fcheshnyey
later	**później**	poozhnyey
half an hour ago	**pół godziny temu**	poow godjeeni
in ten minutes' time	**za dziesięć minut**	za djeshench meenoot
What time is it?	**Która godzina?**	ktoora godjeena
It's ...	**Jest ...**	yest
It's one (o'clock)	**Pierwsza (godzina)**	pyerfsha (godjeena)
It's six (o'clock)	**Jest szósta (godzina)**	yest shoosta (godjeena)
It's a quarter past eight	**Jest piętnaście po ósmej**	yest pyentnashche po oosmey
(At) what time?	**O której godzinie?**	o ktoorey godjeenye
At half past one	**O w pół do drugiej**	o f poow do droogyey
At a quarter to seven	**Za piętnaście siódma**	za pyentnashche shoodma

123

Countries and nationalities

I Nationalities are written with a capital letter. Languages are the same as the masculine adjective form, and are written with a small letter. Remember to change adjective endings to **-a** for feminine nouns and **-e** for neuter and plural nouns.

Country (English name)	Country (Polish name)	Nationality (masculine, feminine and masculine adjective)
Africa	**Afryka**	**Afrykanin, Afrykanka, afrykański**
Albania	**Albania**	**Albańczyk, Albanka, albański**
Algeria	**Algieria**	**Algierczyk, Algierka, algierski**
America	**Ameryka**	**Amerykanin, Amerykanka, amerykański**
Asia	**Azja**	**Azjata, Azjatka, azjatycki**
Australia	**Australia**	**Australijczyk, Australijka, australijski**
Austria	**Austria**	**Austriak, Austriaczka, austriacki**
Basque Country	**Kraj Basków**	**Baskijczyk, Baskijka, baskijski**
Belgium	**Belgia**	**Belgijczyk, Belgijka, belgijski**
Bulgaria	**Bułgaria**	**Bułgar, Bułgarka, bułgarski**
Byelorussia	**Białoruś**	**Białorusin, Białorusinka, białoruski**
Bosnia	**Bośnia**	**Bośniak, Bośniaczka, bośniacki**
Canada	**Kanada**	**Kanadyjczyk, Kanadyjka, kanadyjski**
Catalonia	**Katalonia**	**Katalończyk, Katalonka, kataloński**
Central America	**Ameryka Środkowa**	**Amerykanin/ Amerykanka z** (from) **Ameryki Środkowej, środkowo-amerykański**
China	**Chiny**	**Chińczyk, Chinka, chiński**
Croatia	**Chorwacja**	**Chorwat, Chorwaczka, chorwacki**
Czech Republic	**Czechy**	**Czech, Czeszka, czeski**
Denmark	**Dania**	**Duńczyk, Dunka, duński**

England	Anglia	Anglik, Angielka, angielski
Estonia	Estonia	Estończyk, Estonka, estoński
Europe	Europa	Europejczyk, Europejka, europejski
Finland	Finlandia	Fin, Finka, fiński
France	Francja	Francuz, Francuzka, francuski
Germany	Niemcy	Niemiec, Niemka, niemiecki
Great Britain	Wielka Brytania	Brytyjczyk, Brytyjka, brytyjski
Greece	Grecja	Grek, Greczynka, grecki
Hungary	Węgry	Węgier, Węgierka, węgierski
India	India	Hindus, Hinduska, hinduski
Ireland	Irlandia	Irlandczyk, Irlandka, irlandzki
Israel	Izrael	Izraelita, Izraelitka, izraelski
Italy	Włochy	Włoch, Włoszka, włoski
Japan	Japonia	Japończyk, Japonka, japoński
Latvia	Łotwa	Łotysz, Łotyszka, łotewski
Lithuania	Litwa	Litwin, Litwinka, litewski
Luxembourg	Luksemburg	Luksemburczyk, Luksemburka, luksmburski
Macedonia	Macedonia	Macedończyk, Macedonka, macedoński
Mexico	Meksyk	Meksykanin, Meksykanka, meksykański
Moldavia	Mołdawia	Mołdawianin, Mołdawianka, mołdawski
Morocco	Maroko	Marokańczyk, Marokanka, marokański
Netherlands	Holandia	Holenderczyk, Holenderka, holenderski
New Zealand	Nowa Zelandia	Zelandczyk, Zelandka, nowo-zelandzki
North America	Północna Ameryka	Amerykanin/Amerykanka z (from) Północnej Ameryki, północno-amerykański

125

Northern Ireland	Irlandia Północna	Irlandczyk, Irlandka z (from) Irlandii Północnej, północno-irlandzki
Norway	Norwegia	Norweg, Norweżka, norweski
Poland	Polska	Polak, Polka, polski
Portugal	Portugalia	Portugalczyk, Portugalka, portugalski
Romania	Rumunia	Rumun, Rumunka, rumuński
Russia	Rosja	Rosjanin, Rosjanka, rosyjski
Scotland	Szkocja	Szkot, Szkotka, szkocki
Slovak Republic	Słowacja	Słowak, Słowaczka, słowacki
Slovenia	Słowenia	Słoweniec, Słowenka, słoweński
South America	Południowa Ameryka	Amerykanin/ Amerykanka z (from) Południowej Ameryki, południowo-amerykański
Soviet Union	Związek Radziecki	Rosjanin, Rosjanka, rosyjski
Spain	Hiszpania	Hiszpan, Hiszpanka, hiszpański
Sweden	Szwecja	Szwed, Szwedka, szwedzki
Switzerland	Szwajcaria	Szwajcar, Szwajcarka, szwajcarski
Turkey	Turcja	Turczyn, Turczynka, turecki
Ukraine	Ukraine	Ukrainiec, Ukrainka, ukraiński
United Kingdom	Zjednoczone Królewstwo	
United States	Stany Zednoczone	Amerykanin, Amerykanka, amerykański
Wales	Walia	Walijczyk, Walijka, walijski
West Indies	Indie Zachodnie	Jamajczyk, Jamajka, jamajski
Yugoslavia	Jugosławia	Jugosłowianin, Jugosłowianka, jugosłowiański

To speak a language is: **mówić po polsku, angielsku, hiszpańsku, włosku** etc.

Damski	Ladies (toilet)
Data ważności	Expiry date
Dla niepalących	Non-smokers
Dla palących	Smokers
Dla pań/Dla panów	Ladies/Gentlemen (toilets)
Do wynajęcia	To let
Godziny urzędowania	Office hours
Godziny zwiedzania	Visiting hours
Instrukcja obsługi	Instructions for use
Kasa	Ticket office or Cashier
Kierownictwo zastrzega prawo wstępu	The management reserves the right of admission
Męski	Men (toilets)
Niebezpieczeństwo	Danger
Niebezpieczeństwo pożaru	Fire hazard
Nieczynne	Closed or Out of order
Nie działa	Out of order
Nie blokować wjazdu/wejścia	Do not obstruct entrance
Nie deptać trawników	Keep off the grass
Nie dotykać	Do not touch
Nie działa/Nieczynne	Out of order
Odjazdy	Departures (trains, buses)
Odloty	Departures (flights)
Ogłoszenie	Announcement
Okazje	Bargains
Opóźnienie	Delay
Ostrożnie	Caution/Beware
Otwarte	Open
Palenie wzbronione	No smoking
Parter	Ground floor
Pchnąć	Push
Piętro	Floor (storey)
Piwnica	Basement
Pociągnąć	Pull
Poczekalnia	Waiting-room
Pralnia chemiczna	Dry cleaners
Pranie ręczne	Hand-wash only
Prosimy nie palić	No smoking
Przyjazdy	Arrivals (trains, buses)

Przyloty	Arrivals (planes)
Skrzynka pocztowa	Post-box
Sposób użycia	Instructions for use
Spożyć przed ...	Use by ..
Sprzedaż	For sale
Sprzedaż znaczków pocztowych	Stamps for sale
Strajk	Strike (work)
Strzeż się pociągu	Beware of the trains
Świeżo malowane	Wet paint
Trzymać w chłodnym miejscu	Keep in a cool place
Ubikacja	Toilet
Uwaga	Attention/ Caution/Beware
Uwaga pociąg	Beware of the trains
Uwaga stopień	Mind the step
Uwaga zły pies	Beware of the dog
Wejście	Entrance (on foot)
Wjazd	Entrance (by vehicle)
Wejście wzbronione	No entry
Winda	Lift (elevator)
Woda pitna	Drinking water
Wolne miejsca	Free/Vacant
Wstęp	Admission
Wstęp tylko dla upoważnionych	Admission for authorized persons only
Wstęp wolny	Admission free
Wyjście awaryjne/ zapasowe	Emergency exit
Wyprzedaż	Sale/Reductions
Zajęte	Engaged (occupied)
Zamknięte	Closed
△	Men's toilet
○	Women's toilet

Conversion tables

All measurements are approximate equivalents

Linear measurements

centimetres **centymetry (cm)**
metres **metry (m)**
kilometres **kilometry (km)**

10cm = 4 inches	1 inch = 2.54 cm
50cm = 19.6 inches	1 foot = 30cm
1 metre = 39.37 inches	1 yard = 0.91m
	(just over one yard)
100 metres = 110 yards	
1 km = 0.62 miles	1 mile = 1.61 km

To convert:

km to miles: divide by 8 and multiply by 5
miles to km: divide by 5 and multiply by 8

Miles/Kilometres Conversion

miles		kilometres	miles		kilometres
0.6	1	1.6	19	30	48
1.2	2	3.2	25	40	64
1.9	3	4.8	31	50	80
2.5	4	6.4	62	100	161
3	5	8	68	110	177
6	10	16	75	120	193
12	20	32	81	130	209

Liquid measures

litre **litr (l)**
1 litre = 1.8 pints   1 pint = 0.57 litres
5 litres = 1.1 gallon   1 gallon = 4.55 litres
'A litre of water's a pint and three quarters'

Gallons/Litres

gallons		litres	gallons		litres
0.2	1	4.5	0.9	4	18
0.4	2	9	1.1	5	23
0.7	3	13.6	2.2	10	45.5

Weights

gram **gram**
100 grams **sto gramów**
200 grams **dwieście gramów**
kilo **kilo (kg)**

100 g = 3.5 oz   1 oz = 28 g
200 g = 7 oz   ¼ lb = 113 g
½ kg = 1.1 lb   ½ lb = 227 g
1 kg = 2.2 lb   1 lb = 453 g

Pounds/Kilos Conversion

pounds		kilos	pounds		kilos
2.2	1	0.45 (450)	8.8	4	1.8 (1800)
4.4	2	0.9 (900)	11	5	2.3 (2300)
6.6	3	1.4 (1400)	22	10	4.5 (4500)

Area

hectare **hektar**

1 hectare = 2.5 acres   1 acre = 0.4 hectares

To convert:

hectares to acres: divide by 2 and multiply by 5

acres to hectares: divide by 5 and multiply by 2

Hectares/Acres Conversion

hectares		acres	hectares		acres
0.4	1	2.5	10	25	62
2.0	5	12	20	50	124
4	10	25	40.5	100	247

Clothing and shoe sizes

Women's dresses and suits

UK	10	12	14	16	18	20
Continental	36	38	40	42	44	46

Men's suits and coats

UK	36	38	40	42	44	46
Continental	46	48	50	52	54	56

Men's shirts

UK	14	14½	15	15½	16	16½	17
Continental	36	37	38	39	41	42	43

Shoes

UK	2	3	4	5	6	7	8	9	10	11
Con	35	36	37	38	39	41	42	43	44	45

Waist and chest measurements

in	28	30	32	34	36	38	40	42	44	46	48	50
cm	71	76	81	87	91	97	102	107	112	117	122	127

Tyre pressures

lb/sq in	15	18	20	22	24	26	28	30	33	35
kg/sq cm	1.1	1.3	1.4.	1.5	1.7	1.8	2.0	2.1	2.3	2.5

National holidays

Nowy Rok	New Year's Day	1 January
Wielki Piątek	Good Friday	
Wielkanoc	Easter	
Dzień Pracy	Labour Day	1 May
Rocznica Konstytucji 3 Maja	Constitution Day	3 May
Boże Ciało	Corpus Christi	First Thursday of June
Wniebowzięcie	Assumption	15 August
Wszystkich Świętych	All Saints' Day	1 November
Rocznica Odzyskania Niepodległości	National Independence Day	11 November
Boże Narodzenie	Christmas Day	25 December

Useful addresses

In the UK

Polish Embassy
47 Portland Place
London W1N 3AG
tel: 0171-580-4324/9

Polish Consulate
73 New Cavendish Street
London W1M 7RB
tel: 0171-580-0476

Polish Consulate in Scotland
2 Kinnear Road
Edinburgh EH35 5PE
tel: 0131-552-0301

Polish Cultural Institute
34 Portland Place
London W1N 4HQ
tel: 0171-636-6032/3/4

Polish Social and Cultural Association
238-246 King Street
London W6 ORF
tel: 0181-741-1940

Polorbis Travel Limited
82 Mortimer Street
London W1N 7DE
tel: 0171-637-4971

In Poland

British Embassy
Aleja Róż 1
00-556 Warsaw
tel: 628-10-01/5

British Consulate
ul. Emilii Plater 28
00-688 Warsaw
tel: 625-30-30/32/29

American Embassy
Aleje Ujazdowskie 29/31
00-540 Warsaw
tel: 628-30-41

Canadian Embassy
ul. Matejki 1/5
00-481 Warsaw
tel: 298-051

Irish Embassy
ul. Lenartowicza 18
02-614 Warsaw
tel: 48-01-40
   or: 44-64-40

Australian Embassy
ul. Estońska 3/5
03-903 Warsaw
tel: 17-60-81

In Republic of Ireland

Polish Embassy
12 Ailsbury Road
Dublin 4
tel: 283-0855

In the USA

Polish Embassy
2640 16th Street
NW Washington DC 20009
tel: (202)-234-3800/1/2

Polish National Tourist Board
State 228
333 North Michigan Avenue
Chicago IL 60601
tel: (312)-236-9013

State 1711
275 Madison Avenue
New York NY 10016
tel: (212)-338-9412

▌ The following word lists can be referred to in this book:

types of food – in Menu reader,	page 67
car parts and road signs – in Road travel,	page 24
parts of the body – in Health,	page 90
nationalities – in Countries and nationalities,	page 124

▌ Words which have the same meaning and the same, or very similar, form in English and Polish, are not included.

▌ Most Polish verbs have two forms: imperfect and perfect; in this dictionary only the imperfect form is given.

▌ Most feminine nouns end in **-a**. The feminine forms of nouns will follow the masculine ones where appropriate. Similarly, feminine adjectives end in **-a**, neuter and plural ones in **-e**. The feminine and neuter endings are given after the masculine forms of adjectives.

A

about (on the subject of)	**o**
about (approximately)	**około**
above	**nad**
abroad (to live)	**za granicą**
abroad (to go)	**jechać za granicę**
abscess	**wrzód**
to accept	**przyjmować**
accident	**wypadek**
accommodation	**mieszkanie**

according to	**według**
account (bank)	**konto**
accountant	**księgowy/ księgowa**
ache or pain	**ból**
across (to go across)	**przez**
across (on the other side)	**na drugiej stronie**
to act	**działać**
activity	**działalność**
adaptor (voltage)	**łącznik**
adaptor (multiple plug)	**złodziej, złodziejka**
adhesive tape	**taśma klejąca**

admission	**wstęp**	almond	**migdał**
admission charge	**opłata za wstęp**	alone	**sam/a/e**
adult	**dorosły/a/e**	along	**wzdłuż**
advance (in advance)	**z góry**	already	**już**
		also	**też**
advanced (level)	**zaawansowany /a/e**	although	**chociaż**
		always	**zawsze**
advertisement	**reklama**	am (I am)	**jestem**
aerial	**antena**	ambition	**ambicja**
afford: I can't afford it	**nie stać mnie na to**	ambulance	**pogotowie**
		among	**między**
afraid: to be afraid	**bać się**	amount	**suma**
after	**po**	amusement park	**wesołe miasteczko**
afternoon	**południe**		
after-shave	**płyn po goleniu**	anaesthetic	**narkoza**
again	**znów**	and	**i**
against	**przeciwko**	angling	**wędkarstwo**
age	**wiek**	angry	**zły/a/e**
agency	**agencja**	animal	**zwierzę**
ago	**temu**	anniversary	**rocznica**
to agree	**zgadzać się**	annoyed	**zirytowany/a/e**
AIDS	**Aids**	anorak	**wiatrówka**
air	**powietrze**	another (one)	**inny/a/e/**
air-conditioning	**klimatyzacja**	answer	**odpowiedź**
airline	**linie lotnicze**	to answer	**odpowiadać**
airport	**lotnisko**	antibiotic	**antybiotyk**
alarm clock	**budzik**	anti-freeze	**odmrażacz**
alive	**żywy/a/e**	antique	**antyk**
all	**wszystko**	any (none/neither)	**żadny/a/e**
to allow	**pozwalać**	anyone	**każdy/a/e**
allowed	**zezwala się**	anything (something)	**cokolwiek**
all right	**w porządku**		

anything else?	coś jeszcze?
anyway	w każdym razie
anywhere	gdziekolwiek
apart (from)	oprócz (tego)
apartment	mieszkanie
appendicitis	zapalenie wyrostka robaczkowego
apple	jabłko
appointment	spotkanie
approximately	w przybliżeniu
apricot	morela
arch	łuk
are (they are)	są
area (surface)	powierzchnia
area (region)	obszar
argument (quarrel)	kłótnia
army	armia or wojsko
around	wokół
around the corner	za rogiem
to arrange	organizować
to arrest	aresztować
arrival (by road)	przyjazd
arrival (by air)	przylot
to arrive (by foot)	przyjść
to arrive (by road)	przyjechać
to arrive (by air)	przylecieć
art/fine arts	sztuka/sztuki piękne
art gallery	galeria sztuki
article	artykuł
artificial	sztuczny/a/e

as (comparing things)	jak
as far as	do
ashtray	popielniczka
to ask	prosić
as well	też
at (place)	w
at (time)	o
to attack	atakować
aunt	ciotka
autumn	jesień
avalanche	lawina
to avoid	unikać
away: (... kilometres away)	... kilometrów stąd
awful	okropny/a/e

B

baby	niemowlę
baby cereal	kaszka dla dzieci
baby food	jedzenie dla dzieci
baby's bottle	butelka dziecka
babysitter	ktoś do pilnowania dziecka
back: at the back	z tyłu
backwards	do tyłu
bacon	boczek
bad	zły/a/e
badly	źle

bag	**torba**	behind	**za**
baker	**piekarz**	to believe	**wierzyć**
baker's	**piekarnia**	bell	**dzwonek**
ball	**piłka**	bell (church)	**dzwon**
ballpoint pen	**długopis**	to belong to	**należeć do**
band (music)	**zespół**	below	**pod**
barber's	**fryzjer**	belt	**pasek**
basement	**piwnica**	bend	**zakręt**
basket	**koszyk**	bent	**zgięty/a/e**
basketball	**koszykówka**	berth	**koja**
bath (tub)	**wanna**	beside (next to)	**koło**
bathing	**kąpiel**	besides	**oprócz**
to have a bath	**kąpać się**	best (adverb)	**najlepiej**
bathing costume	**kostium kąpielowy**	better (adverb/ adjective)	**lepiej/ lepszy/a/e**
bathroom	**łazienka**	between	**między**
bay	**zatoka**	beyond	**poza**
to be	**być**	bicycle	**rover**
beach	**plaża**	big	**duży/a/e**
bean	**fasola**	bigger	**większy/a/e**
beard	**broda**	bill	**rachunek**
beautiful	**piękny/a/e**	bin	**kosz na śmieci**
because	**bo** or **ponieważ**	binoculars	**lornetka**
bed	**łóżko**	bird	**ptak**
bedroom	**sypialnia**	birthday	**urodziny**
bee	**pszczoła**	biscuit	**herbatnik**
before	**przed**	bishop	**biskup**
to begin	**zaczynać**	a bit	**kawałek**
beginner	**początkujący/ a/e**	to bite	**gryźć**
		bitter	**gorzki/a/e**
beginning	**początek**	black	**czarny/a/e**

black and white (film)	**czarno-biały**	boot (car)	**bagażnik**
		border	**granica**
black coffee	**czarna kawa**	bored	**znudzony/a/e**
blackcurrant	**czarna porzeczka**	boring	**nudny/a/e**
		both	**oboje** or **jedno i drugie**
blanket	**koc**		
bleach	**wybielacz**		
to bleed	**krwawić**	bottle	**butelka**
blind (eyes)	**niewidomy/a/e**	bottle opener	**otwieracz butelki**
blind (window)	**zasłona**		
blister	**pęcherz**	bottom (of the river, etc.)	**dno**
blocked	**zablokowany/a/e**	bow (ship)	**dziób**
		bow (knot)	**węzeł**
blood	**krew**	bowl	**miska**
blouse	**bluzka**	box	**pudełko**
blow-dry	**wysuszyć suszarką**	box (theatre)	**loża**
		box office	**kasa** or **sprzedaż biletów**
blue	**niebieski/a/e**		
boarding (a plane)	**wsiadanie**		
boarding card	**karta lotu**	boy	**chłopiec**
boat (small)	**łódź**	boyfriend	**chłopak**
boat (big)	**statek**	brain	**mózg**
by boat	**statkiem**	branch (bank)	**oddział**
body	**ciało**	branch (tree)	**gałęź**
boiled	**gotowany/a/e**	brand	**gatunek**
bone	**kość**	brandy	**koniak**
book	**książka**	brass	**mosiądz**
booking	**rezerwacja**	brave	**odważny/a/e**
booking office (railway, etc.)	**sprzedaż biletów** or **kasa**	bread	**chleb**
		to break	**łamać**
bookshop	**księgarnia**	I have broken ...	**złamałem/ złamałam ...**
boot (wellington)	**kalosz**		

breakdown truck	**pojazd pomocy drogowej**	bush	**krzak**
breakfast	**śniadanie**	business studies	**studia handlowe**
to breathe	**oddychać**	business trip	**służbowo**
bricklayer	**ceglarz**	bus station	**stacja autobusowa**
bride	**panna młoda**	bus stop	**przystanek autobusowy**
bridegroom	**pan młody**		
bridge (over the river)	**most**	busy	**zajęty/a/e**
briefcase	**teczka**	but	**ale**
bright (colour)	**żywy/a/e**	butane gas	**butan**
bright (light)	**jasny/a/e**	butcher's	**rzeźnik**
to bring	**przynieść**	butter	**masło**
broad	**szeroki/a/e**	butterfly	**motyl**
broken	**złamany/a/e**	button	**guzik**
brother	**brat**	to buy	**kupować**
brother-in-law	**szwagier**		
brown	**brązowy/a/e**	**C**	
brown sugar	**brązowy cukier**	cabbage	**kapusta**
bruise	**siniak**	cabin	**kabina**
brush	**pędzel**	café	**kawiarnia**
bucket	**wiadro**	call (phone)	**telefon**
to build	**budować**	to call (phone)	**dzwonić**
building	**budynek**	to call (visit)	**odwiedzać**
bulb (electric)	**żarówka**	to be called	**nazywać się**
bull	**byk**	I am called	**nazywam się**
burn	**oparzenie**	he/she/it is called	**on/ona/ono nazywa się**
to burn (with something hot)	**oparzyć się**	what is he/she/it called?	**jak on/ona/ono nazywa się?**
to burn (cooking)	**palić**		
bus	**autobus**		
by bus	**autobusem**	calm	**spokojny/a/e**

camera	aparat fotograficzny	carriage (railway)	wagon
to camp	rozbijać obóz	carrot	marchew
campbed	łóżko polowe	to carry	nieść
campsite	pole kampingowe	car wash	myjnia samochodów
can (to be able to do something)	móc	case: just in case	na wszelki wypadek
can (to know how to do sthg.)	umieć	cash: to pay by cash	płacić gotówką
		to cash	zrealizować czek
can/tin	puszka	cash desk	okienko
can opener	otwieracz do puszek	castle	zamek
		cat	kot
to cancel	odwołać	to catch	łapać
cancer	rak	cauliflower	kalafior
candle	świeca	to cause	powodować
canoe	kajak	cave	jaskinia
capital city	stolica	ceiling	sufit
car	samochód	celery	seler
by car	samochodem	cemetery	cmentarz
caravan	wóz kampingowy	central heating	centralne ogrzewanie
caravan site	pole kampingowe	century	wiek
		cereal	kaszka
cardigan	sweter	certain	pewny/a/e
care: to take care	być ostrożnym	certainly	na pewno
care	opieka	certificate	zaświadczenie
careful	ostrożny/a/e	chain	łańcuch
careless	nieostrożny/a/e	chair	krzesło
car park	parking	chairlift	wyciąg krzesełkowy
carpenter	cieślarz		
carpet	dywan	change (small coins)	drobne

to change	zmieniać	Christian name	imię
to change clothes	przebierać się	Christmas	Boże Narodzenie
changing room	przebieralnia		
channel	kanał	Christmas Eve	Wigilia
chapel	kaplica	church	kościół
charge	opłata	cigar	cygaro
charter flight	lot czarterowy	cigarette	papieros
cheap	tani/a/e	cigarette lighter	zapalniczka
to check	kontrolować	cinema	kino
check-in (desk)	odprawa	circle	koło
to check in	zgłosić się do odprawy	circle (theatre)	balkon
		circus	cyrk
cheek	policzek	city	miasto
cheeky	bezczelny/a/e	civil servant	urzędnik państwowy/ urzędniczka państwowa
cheers! (hello!)	cześć!		
cherry	czereśnia		
chess	szachy		
chestnut	kasztan	clean	czysty/a/e
chewing gum	guma do żucia	to clean	czyścić
chickenpox	wietrzna ospa	cleansing cream	krem oczyszczający
child	dziecko		
children	dzieci	clear	jasny/a/e
chimney	komin	clerk	urzędnik/ urzędniczka
china	porcelana		
chips	frytki	clever	mądry/a/e
chocolate	czekolada	cliff	skała
chocolates (box)	czekoladki	climate	klimat
to choose	wybierać	to climb (up)	wspinać się
chop (meat)	kotlet	climber	alpinista
Christian	chrześcijanin/ chrześcijanka	climbing	wspinaczka
		cloakroom	szatnia or garderoba

clock	**zegar**	college (further/ higher education)	**szkoła wyższa/ uniwersytet**
close (near)	**blisko**	colour blind	**daltonista**
to close	**zamykać**	comb	**grzebień**
closed	**zamknięty/a/e**	to come	**przychodzić**
cloth (for cleaning)	**ścierka**	are you coming? (on foot)	**przychodzisz?**
clothes	**odzież**	to come back	**wracać**
cloud	**chmura**	to come in	**wchodzić**
cloudy	**zachmurzone**	come in!	**proszę wejść!**
coach (bus)	**autokar**	comfortable	**wygodny/a/e**
coach (railway)	**wagon**	common (ground)	**wspólny/a/e**
coal	**węgiel**	company (firm)	**firma**
coarse	**szorstki/a/e**	compared with	**w porównaniu z**
coast	**wybrzeże**	compartment	**przedział**
coat (short)/(long)	**kurtka/płaszcz**	to complain	**skarżyć się**
coat hanger	**wieszak**	make a complaint	**złożyć reklamację**
coin	**moneta**	completely	**całkowicie**
cold	**zimny/a/e**	complicated	**skomplikowany /a/e**
I'm cold	**zimno mi**		
it's cold	**zimno**	compulsory	**obowiązkowy/a /e**
I've got a cold	**jestem przeziębiony/a**	computer science	**nauka o komputerach**
collar	**kołnierz**	concert hall	**sala koncertowa**
collar (dog's)	**smycz**		
colleague (male/ female)	**kolega/ koleżanka**	concussion	**wstrząs mózgu**
to collect	**zbierać**	condition (of doing something)	**warunek**
collection	**kolekcja**		
collection (letters)	**wybieranie listów**	condition (physical state)	**kondycja**
collection (rubbish)	**wybieranie śmieci**	conditioner (hair)	**odżywka do włosów**

to confirm	potwierdzać	cotton (thread)	nitka
connection (travel)	połączenie	cotton wool	wata
conscious	świadomy/a/e	cough	kaszleć
conservation	konserwacja	cough medicine	syrop na kaszel
constipation	zatwardzenie	to count	liczyć
to contact	kontaktować	counter (shop)	lada
I want to contact ...	chcę się skontaktować z ...	country (nation)	kraj
		countryside	wieś
contact lenses	szkła kontaktowe	couple (things)	parę
		couple (people)	para
contraceptive	środek antykoncepcyjny	courgette	cukinia
		course (lessons)	kurs
		course (meal)	danie
convenient	wygodny/a/e	court (law)	sąd
it's not convenient	nie pasuje	court (yard)	dziedziniec
cook	kucharz/ kucharka	court (sport)	kort
		cousin	kuzyn/kuzynka
cooker	kuchenka	cover	przykrycie
cool	chłodny/a/e	cover charge	opłata za wstęp
copper (metal)	miedź	cow	krowa
cork	korek	cramp (medical)	skurcz
corner	róg	crash (car)	wypadek
correct	właściwy/a/e	crayon	kredka
corridor	korytarz	crazy	wariat
cost	koszt	cream	krem
to cost	kosztować	crisps	frytki
how much does it cost?	ile to kosztuje?	cross	krzyż
		to cross (road, on foot)	przechodzić
cot	łóżeczko		
cottage	domek	to cross (in a vehicle)	przejechać
cotton (material)	bawełna		

cross-country skiing	**narciarstwo biegowe**
crossing (sea)	**przeprawa promem**
crossroads	**skrzyżowanie**
crowded	**tłok**
crown	**korona**
cruise	**wycieczka morska**
to cry (weep)	**płakać**
to cry (shout)	**krzyczeć**
cucumber	**ogórek**
cup	**filiżanka**
cupboard	**szafka**
cure (remedy)	**lekarstwo**
to cure	**leczyć**
curling tongs	**elektryczne wałki**
curly	**kręcony/a/e**
current (electric)	**prąd**
curtain	**zasłona**
curve	**zakręt**
cushion	**poduszka**
custard	**budyń**
customs (office)	**urząd celny**
customs (traditions)	**obyczaje** or **tradycje**
cut	**skaleczenie**
to cut	**ciąć**
cutlery	**sztućce**
cycling	**jazda na rowerze**

cyclist	**rowerzysta/ rowerzystka**
cystitis	**zapalenie pęcherza**

D

daily	**codziennie**
damaged	**uszkodzony/a/e**
damp	**wilgotny/a/e**
dance	**taniec**
to dance	**tańczyć**
danger	**niebez- pieczeństwo**
dangerous	**niebezpieczny/ a/e**
dark	**ciemny/a/e**
darling	**kochany/a/e**
darts	**strzałki**
data (information)	**dane**
date (day)	**data**
date (fruit)	**daktyl**
date (meeting)	**spotkanie**
daughter	**córka**
daughter-in-law	**synowa**
day	**dzień**
day after tomorrow	**pojutrze**
day before yesterday	**przedwczoraj**
dead	**nieżywy/a/e**
deaf	**głuchy**
dealer	**handlarz/ handlarka**
dear (loved)	**kochany/a/e**

dear (expensive)	**drogi/a/e**	design	**project**
death	**śmierć**	designer	**projektant/ projektantka**
debt	**dług**		
decaffeinated	**bez kafeiny**	dessert	**deser**
to decide	**decydować**	destination (travel)	**cel podróży**
deck	**pokład**	detail	**szczegół**
deckchair	**leżak**	detergent	**środek do prania**
deep	**głęboki/a/e**		
deep freeze	**zamrażarka**	to develop	**rozwijać**
deer	**jeleń**	diabetes	**cukrzyca**
defect	**wada**	to dial	**wykręcić numer**
definitely	**zdecydowanie**		
to defrost	**odmrozić**	dialling code	**numer kodu**
degree (temperature)	**stopień**	dialling tone	**sygnał**
degree (university)	**dyplom**	diamond	**diament**
delay	**opóźnienie**	diarrhoea	**rozwolnienie**
delicious (taste)	**pyszny/a/e**	diary	**dziennik**
dentures	**sztuczne szczęki**	dice	**kostka**
		dictionary	**słownik**
to depart (on foot)	**odchodzić**	to die	**umierać**
to depart (by road)	**odjeżdżać**	he/she died	**on umarł/ona umarła**
to depart (by plane)	**odlecieć**		
department	**wydział**	diet	**dieta**
departure (by foot)	**odejście**	different	**inny/a/e**
departure (by road)	**odjazd**	difficult	**trudny/a/e**
departure (by plane)	**odlot**	dining room	**jadalnia**
departure lounge	**sala dla pasażerów**	dinner	**obiad**
		direct	**bezpośredni/ a/e**
to describe	**opisywać**		
description	**opis**	direction	**kierunek**
desert	**pustynia**	directory (telephone)	**książka telefoniczna**

dirty	brudny/a/e	double	podwójny/a/e
disabled	inwalida/ inwalidka	double bed	podwójne łóżko
		dough	ciasto
disappointed	rozczarowany/ a/e	down	w dole
		downstairs	na dole
discount	redukcja	drain	drenaż
dish	naczynie	draught	susza
dishwasher	maszyna do zmywania naczyń	to draw (a picture)	rysować
		drawer (in chest of drawers)	szuflada
disinfectant	dezynfektant		
dislocated	zwichnięty/a/e	drawing	rysunek
disposable nappies	pieluszki jednorazowe	drawing pin	pineska
		dreadful	okropny/a/e
distance	odległość	dress	suknia
distilled water	woda destylowana	dressing (medical)	opatrunek
		dressing (salad)	oliwka
district (city)	dzielnica	drink	coś do picia
to dive	nurkować	to drink	pić
diversion (road)	objazd	to drip	cieknąć
diving board	trampolina	to drive	prowadzić samochód
divorced	rozwiedziony/ a/e		
		driver	kierowca
dizzy	mieć zawrót głowy	driving licence	prawo jazdy
		drowned	utopiony/a/e
to do	robić	drug	narkotyk
docks	doki	drug addict	narkoman/ narkomanka
doctor	lekarz or doktór		
dog	pies	drum	bęben
doll	lalka	drunk	pijany/a/e
dome	kopuła	dry (weather)	suchy/a/e
donkey	osioł	dry (wine)	wytrawne
door	drzwi		

dry cleaner's	pralnia chemiczna	election	wybory
		electrician	elektryk
dubbed (film)	zdubingowany	else: everything else	wszystko inne
duck (bird)	kaczka	embarrassing	kłopotliwy/a/e
dull (weather)	pochmurnie	embassy	ambasada
dumb	niemy/a/e	emergency	nagły wypadek
dummy (baby's)	smoczek	empty	pusty/a/e
during	podczas	to empty (rubbish)	wyrzucać
dust	kurz	enamel	emalia
dusty	zakurzony/a/e	end	koniec
duty (customs)	cło	to end	kończyć
duty-free	wolne od cła	energetic	energiczny/a/e
duvet	kołdra	engaged (occupied)	zajęty/a/e
		engaged (to be married)	zaręczony/a/e

E

		engine	silnik
each	każdy/a/e	engineer	inżynier
ear	ucho	enough	dosyć
earache	ból ucha	to enter	wchodzić
earlier	wcześniej	entertainment	rozrywka
early	wczesny/a/e	entrance	wejście
to earn	zarabiać	envelope	koperta
earring	kolczyk	environment	środowisko
earth	ziemia	equal	równy/a/e
earthquake	trzęsienie ziemi	equipment	sprzęt
east	wschód	escalator	ruchome schody
Easter	Wielkanoc		
easy	łatwy/a/e	especially	specjalnie
to eat	jeść	essential	bardzo ważny/a/e
economical	oszczędny/a/e		
either ... or ...	albo ... albo ...	estate (residential area)	osiedle
elastic band	gumka		

149

evaporated milk	mleko skondensowane
even (including)	nawet
even (not odd)	parzysty/a/e
evening	wieczór
evening dress	suknia wieczorowa
every (each)	każdy/a/e
every (all)	wszyscy
everyone	każdy/a/e
everything	wszystko
everywhere	wszędzie
exactly	dokładnie
exam	egzamin
examination (medical)	badanie
example	przykład
for example	na przykład
excellent	świetny/a/e
except	z wyjątkiem
excess baggage	bagaż z nadwagą
to exchange	wymienić
exchange rate	kurs wymiany
excited	podniecony/a/e
exciting	fascynujący/a/e
excursion	wycieczka
excuse me	przepraszam
executive (power)	wykonawczy/a/e
exercise	ćwiczenie

exhibition	wystawa
exit	wyjście
to expect	oczekiwać
expensive	drogi/a/e
experience	doświadczenie
to explain	wyjaśniać
extension (electric)	przedłużacz
external	zewnętrzny/a/e
extra (in addition)	dodatkowo
eye	oko
eyebrow	brew
eyelash	rzęsa
eye-liner	ołówek do rzęs
eye-shadow	cień do rzęs

F

fabric	materiał
face	twarz
face cream	krem do twarzy
face powder	puder
facilities (not toilets)	ułatwienia
fact	fakt
in fact	właściwie
factory	fabryka
to fail (exam)	nie zdać
failure	porażka
faint: fainted	zemdlony/a/e
fair	targ
fair (hair)	jasny/a/e
trade fair	targi
fairly (quite)	dosyć

faith	**wiara**
faithful	**wierny/a/e**
fake	**fałszywy/a/e**
fall	**upadek**
he/she had a fall	**on upadł/ona upadła**
false (untrue)	**fałszywy/a/e**
false (teeth)	**sztuczny/a/e**
family	**rodzina**
famous	**sławny/a/e**
fan (supporter)	**kibic**
fan (electric)	**wachlarz**
far (away)	**daleko**
is it far?	**czy to daleko?**
fare	**cena biletu**
farm	**gospodarstwo**
farmer	**rolnik**
fashion	**moda**
fashionable	**modny/a/e**
fast	**szybki/a/e**
fat (excess weight)	**gruby/a/e**
fat (large)	**duży/a/e**
father	**ojciec**
father-in-law	**teść**
fault	**wada**
faulty	**z wadą**
favourite	**ulubiony/a/e**
feather	**pióro**
fed up: I'm fed up	**mam dosyć**
to feed	**karmić**
to feel	**czuć**

I feel well/ill	**czuję się dobrze/źle**
felt-tip pen	**flamaster**
female	**płci żeńskiej**
feminine (grammatically)	**żeński**
feminine (womanly)	**kobiecy/a/e**
fence	**płot**
ferry	**prom**
fever	**gorączka**
few	**mało**
a few	**trochę**
fiancée	**narzeczony/a**
fibre	**włókno**
field	**pole**
fight (struggle)	**walka**
fight (quarrel)	**kłótnia**
file (on someone)	**teczka**
file (nail or DIY)	**pilnik**
filling (tooth)	**plomba**
filling (food)	**nadzienie**
film star	**gwiazda filmowa/ gwiazdor filmowy**
to find	**znajdywać**
fine (weather)	**ładna**
fine (penalty)	**mandat**
to finish	**kończyć**
fire (flame)	**ogień**
fire (on fire)	**pożar**

fire brigade	**straż pożarna**	flour	**mąka**
fire extinguisher	**gaśnica**	flu	**grypa**
firewood	**drewno**	fluid	**płyn**
fireworks	**fajerwerki**	fly	**mucha**
firm (company)	**firma** or **przedsiębior-stwo**	foam	**piana**
		fog	**mgła**
first	**pierwszy/a/e**	foggy	**mglisty/a/e**
first aid	**pierwsza pomoc**	folding (chair, etc.)	**składane**
		following (next)	**następny/a/e**
fish	**ryba**	food	**jedzenie** or **żywność**
to fish: to go fishing	**iść na ryby**		
fishing	**wędkarstwo**	food poisoning	**zatrucie pokarmowe**
fishing rod	**wędka**		
fishmonger's	**rybny (sklep)**	foot	**stopa**
fit (healthy)	**w dobrej kondycji**	on foot	**piechotą**
		football	**piłka nożna**
to fit (to be suitable)	**pasować**	footpath	**ścieżka**
fitting room	**przymierzalnia**	for (preposition)	**dla**
to fix	**naprawiać**	forbidden	**wzbroniony/a/e**
fizzy	**z gazem**	foreign	**zagraniczny/a/e**
flag	**flaga**	forest	**las**
flat (apartment)	**mieszkanie**	to forget	**zapominać**
flat (level)	**płaski/a/e**	to forgive	**przebaczać**
flavour	**smak**	fork	**widelec**
flaw	**defekt**	form (document)	**formularz**
flea	**pchła**	fortnight	**dwa tygodnie**
flight	**lot**	forward (direction)	**do przodu**
flippers	**płetwy**	foundation (make-up)	**krem pod makijaż**
flood	**powódź**		
floor	**podłoga**	fracture	**pęknięcie**
floor (storey)	**piętro**	fragile	**delikatny/a/e**
		frankly	**otwarcie**

freckle, freckles	**plamka, piegi**
free (gratis)	**darmo**
free (available)	**wolny/a/e**
freedom	**wolność**
to freeze	**zamarzać**
freezer	**zamrażarka**
frequent	**częsty/a/e**
fresh	**świeży/a/e**
fridge	**lodówka**
fried	**smażony/a/e**
friend	**przyjaciel/ przyjaciółka**
frightened	**przerażony/a/e**
fringe (hair)	**grzywka**
frog	**żaba**
from	**z** or **od**
front: in front of	**z przodu**
front door	**drzwi wejściowe**
frontier	**granica**
frost	**mróz**
frozen	**zamarznięty/a/e**
fruit	**owoc**
frying pan	**patelnia**
fuel	**paliwo**
full	**pełny/a/e**
full board	**pełne wyżywienie**
full up	**brak miejsc**
funeral	**pogrzeb**
funfair	**wesołe miasteczko**

funny (amusing)	**zabawny/a/e**
funny (peculiar)	**śmieszny/a/e**
fur	**futro**
furniture	**meble**
further on	**dalej**
fuse	**bezpiecznik**

G

gallery	**galeria**
gambling	**gry hazardowe**
game (sport or board)	**gra**
game (match)	**mecz**
game (meat)	**dziczyzna**
garden	**ogród**
gardener	**ogrodnik/ ogrodniczka**
garlic	**czosnek**
gas bottle	**butla z gazem**
gas refill	**gaz zapasowy**
gastritis	**nieżyt żołądka**
gate	**brama**
general (military)	**generał**
general (adjective)	**ogólny/a/e**
generous	**hojny/a/e**
gentle	**łagodny/a/e**
gentleman	**pan**
genuine	**autentyczny/a/e**
to get (obtain)	**dostawać**
to get off	**wysiadać**
to get on	**wsiadać**

gift (present)	**prezent**	goodnight	**dobranoc**
girl	**dziewczyna**	government	**rząd**
girlfriend	**dziewczyna**	grammar	**gramatyka**
to give	**dawać**	grandchildren	**wnuki**
can you give me ...?	**czy może mi pan/pani dać ...?**	granddaughter	**wnuczka**
		grandfather	**dziadek**
glass (container)	**szklanka**	grandmother	**babcia**
glass (material)	**szkło**	grandparents	**dziadkowie**
glasses (spectacles)	**okulary**	grandson	**wnuk**
glove	**rękawiczka**	grape	**winogrono**
glue	**klej**	grapefruit	**grejpfrut**
to go	**chodzić**	grass	**trawa**
let's go (on foot)	**chodźmy**	grateful	**wdzięczny/a/e**
let's go (by transport)	**jedźmy**	greasy (covered in grease)	**tłusty/a/e**
to go down	**schodzić**	great	**wielki/a/e**
to go in	**wchodzić**	great!	**świetnie!**
to go out	**wychodzić**	green	**zielony/a/e**
to go up (on foot)	**wchodzić**	green card (insurance certificate)	**zielona karta**
to go up (by transport)	**wjeżdżać**	greengrocer's	**sklep warzywny**
goal (sport)	**gol**	to greet	**witać**
goal (aim)	**cel**	grey	**szary/a/e**
goat	**koza**	grilled	**z rusztu**
God	**Bóg**	grocer's	**spożywczy**
gold	**złoto**	ground (earth)	**ziemia**
made of gold	**złoty/a/e**	ground floor	**parter**
good	**dobry/a/e**	groundsheet	**podkładka**
good afternoon/ evening	**dobry wieczór**	group	**grupa**
goodbye	**do widzenia**	to grow	**rosnąć**
good morning	**dzień dobry**	guarantee	**gwarancja**

guest	gość	half board	częściowe wyżywienie
guest house	pensjonat		
guide	przewodnik/ przewodniczka	half price	pół ceny
		hall (in house)	korytarz
guidebook	przewodnik	hall (concert)	sala koncertowa
guided tour	wycieczka z przewodnikiem		
		hammer	młotek
guilty	winny/a/e	handbag	torebka
guitar	gitara	hand cream	krem do rąk
gun	rewolwer	handicapped	inwalida/ inwalidka

H

		handkerchief	chusteczka
habit (custom)	zwyczaj	handle (door)	klamka
haemorrhoids	hemoroidy	handle (cup)	ucho
hail	grad	hand luggage	bagaż ręczny
hair	włosy	handmade	ręcznie robiony/a/e
hairbrush	szczotka do włosów		
		hangover	kac
hair curlers	wałki do włosów	to hang (up)	wieszać
haircut	ostrzyżenie or fryzura	to happen	stawać się
		what has happened?	co się stało?
hairdresser's	fryzjer/fryzjerka	happy	szczęśliwy/a/e
hair dryer	suszarka do włosów	harbour	przystań
		hard (firm)	twardy/a/e
hairgrip	spinka do włosów	hard (difficult)	trudny/a/e
		hat	kapelusz
hair spray	lakier do włosów	to hate	nienawidzieć
		to have	mieć
half	połowa	do you have ...?	czy masz ...? (informal)/ czy pan/pani ma ...? (formal)
half an hour	pół godziny		
half past ... (see Time, page 122)	w pół do ...		

hay fever	**katar sienny**	about her	**o niej**
hazelnut	**orzech laskowy**	with her	**z nią**
he	**on**	herb	**zioło**
head (boss)	**szef/szefowa**	here	**tutaj** or **tu**
head (school)	**dyrektor/ dyrektorka**	hiccoughs	**czkawka**
		(to have hiccoughs)	**mieć czkawkę**
headache	**ból głowy**	high	**wysoki/a/e**
headphones	**słuchawki**	high chair	**wysokie krzesełko**
to heal	**leczyć**		
health	**zdrowie**	to hijack	**uprowadzać**
health foods	**jedzenie zdrowotne**	hill	**wzgórze**
		hill-walking	**chodzenie po górach**
healthy	**zdrowy/a/e**		
to hear	**słuchać**	him	**jemu**
hearing aid	**aparat do słyszenia**	about him	**o nim**
		with him	**z nim**
heart attack	**atak serca**	to hire	**wynajmować**
heat	**gorąco**	his	**jego**
heater	**grzejnik**	to hit	**uderzać**
heating	**ogrzewanie**	to hitch-hike	**jechać autostopem**
heaven	**niebo**		
heavy	**ciężki/a/e**	hole	**dziura**
hedge	**żywopłot**	holiday(s) (school)	**urlop** or **wakacje**
heel (foot)	**pięta**		
heel (shoe)	**obcas**	on holiday	**na urlopie/na wakacjach**
height	**wysokość**		
hell	**piekło**	public holiday	**dzień wolny od pracy**
hello	**dzień dobry** or **cześć**		
		holy	**święty/a/e**
help	**pomoc**	home	**dom**
to help	**pomagać**	at home	**w domu**
her	**jej**	to go home	**iść do domu**

156

...ome address	adres zamieszkania
...onest	uczciwy/a/e
...oneymoon	podróż poślubna
...o hope	mieć nadzieję
...hope so	mam nadzieję
...hope not	mam nadzieję że nie
...orrible	okropny/a/e
...orse	koń
...orse riding	jazda konna
...ose	wąż
...ospital	szpital
...ot (temperature)	gorący/a/e
...'m hot	gorąco mi
...t's hot (weather)	gorąco
...ot (spicy)	pikantny/a/e
...our	godzina
...ouse	dom
...ousewife	gospodyni domowa
...ousework	praca w domu
...overcraft	poduszkowiec
...how?	jak?
...how are you? (informal)	jak się masz?
...how are you? (formal)	co u pana/pani słychać?
...how long? (adverb)	jak długo?
...how many/much?	ile?
...how much is it?	ile to kosztuje?

human	ludzki/a/e
hungry	głodny/a/e
to be hungry	być głodnym/ą
to hunt	polować
hunting	polowanie
hurry	pośpiech
to be in a hurry	spieszyć się
to hurt (someone)	ranić
to hurt: my ... hurts	boli mnie ...
husband	mąż
hut	chata
hydrofoil	wodolot

I

I	ja
ice	lód
ice cream	lody
ice rink	lodowisko
icy	lodowaty/a/e
idea	myśl
if	jeżeli
ill	chory/a/e
illness	choroba
imagination	wyobraźnia
to imagine	wyobrażać sobie
immediately	natychmiast
immersion heater	grzejnik nurkowy
impatient	niecierpliwy/a/e
important	ważny/a/e

impossible	**niemożliwy/a/e**
impressive	**robiący/a/e wrażenie**
in	**w**
included	**łącznie z ...**
income	**dochód**
independent	**niezależny/a/e**
indigestion	**niestrawność**
indoors	**w środku**
industrial	**przemysłowy/a/e**
infected	**zarażony/a/e**
infection	**infekcja**
infectious	**zaraźliwy/a/e**
inflamed	**zaogniony/a/e**
inflammation	**zapalenie**
influenza	**grypa**
informal	**nieoficjany/a/e**
information office	**biuro informacji**
injection	**zastrzyk**
injured	**ranny/a/e**
injury	**rana**
ink	**atrament**
inner	**wewnętrzny/a/e**
innocent	**niewinny/a/e**
insect	**owad**
insect bite	**ukąszenie owada**
insecticide	**środek owadobójczy**

insect repellent	**środek na owady**
inside	**w środku**
to insist	**nalegać**
instant coffee	**kawa rozpuszczalna (neska)**
instead of	**zamiast**
instructor	**instruktor/ isnstruktorka**
insult	**obelga**
insurance	**ubezpieczenie**
insurance certificate	**zaświadczenie o ubezpieczeniu**
interested: I'm (not) interested	**(nie) interesuje mnie**
interesting	**ciekawy/a/e**
interior	**wnętrze**
internal	**wewnętrzny/a/e**
international	**międzynaro- dowy/a/e**
interpreter	**tłumacz/ tłumaczka**
interval (theatre, etc.)	**przerwa**
interview	**rozmowa**
into	**do**
to introduce	**przedstawiać**
to invite	**zapraszać**
invitation	**zaproszenie**
iodine	**jodyna**
iron (metal)	**żelazo**
iron (for clothes)	**żelazko**

to iron	prasować	jug	dzbanek
ironmonger's	sklep z gospodarstwem domowym	juice	sok
		to jump	skakać
		jump leads	mostek
is	jest	jumper	sweter
he/she/it is	on/ona/ono jest	junction	skrzyżowanie
is there ...?	czy jest ...?	just (only)	ledwo
island	wyspa		
it	to	**K**	
itch	swędzenie		
		to keep	trzymać
J		kettle	czajnik
		key	klucz
jacket	żakiet	key-ring	kółko do kluczy
jam	dżem	to kill	zabijać
jar	słoik	kilo(gram)	kilo(gram)
jeans	dżinsy	kilometre	kilometr
Jesus/Jesus Christ	Jezus/Jezus Chrystus	kind (person)	dobry/a/e
		kind (sort)	rodzaj
jelly	galaretka	king	król
jellyfish	meduza	kiss	pocałunek
jeweller's	jubiler	to kiss	całować
Jewish (noun)	Żyd/Żydówka	kitchen	kuchnia
job	praca	knickers	majtki
jogging: to go jogging	biegać	knife	nóż
		to knit	robić na drutach
I go jogging	biegam		
joke	żart	to knock	pukać
journalist	dziennikarz/ dziennikarka	knot	węzeł
		to know (someone)	znać (kogoś)
journey	podróż	I don't know him/her	nie znam jego/jej
judge	sędzia		

to know (to have knowledge of)	**wiedzieć**
I (don't) know	**(nie) wiem**
to know how to	**umieć**
I (don't) know how to	**(nie) umiem**

L

label	**nalepka**
lace (cloth)	**koronka**
lace (shoe)	**sznurowadło**
ladder	**drabina**
lady	**pani**
ladies and gentlemen	**panie i panowie**
lager	**piwo jasne**
lake	**jezioro**
lamb (meat)	**baranina**
lamp-post	**latarnia uliczna**
land	**ziemia**
to land	**lądować**
landlady	**właścicielka**
landlord	**właściciel**
lane (country road)	**droga wiejska**
language	**język**
large	**duży/a/e**
last	**ostatni/a/e**
to last	**trwać**
late	**późny/a/e**
it's late	**jest późno**
later	**później**
laugh	**śmiech**

to laugh	**śmiać się**
launderette	**pralnia**
laundry	**pranie**
law	**prawo**
lawyer	**prawnik/ prawniczka**
laxative	**środek przeczysz- czający**
lazy	**leniwy/a/e**
to lead	**prowadzić** or **przewodzić**
lead (metal)	**ołów**
lead-free	**bezołowiowy/ a/e**
leaf	**liść**
leaflet	**ulotka**
to learn	**uczyć się**
learner	**student/ studentka**
least: at least	**przynajmniej**
leather	**skóra**
to leave (message, etc.)	**zostawiać**
to leave (to go away: on foot/by transport)	**wyjść/wyjechać**
left	**lewy/a/e**
to the left	**na lewo**
on the left-hand side	**po lewej stronie**
left hand	**lewa ręka**
left-handed	**leworęczny/a/e**
legal	**prawny/a/e**

lemon	**cytryna**
lemonade	**lemoniada**
to lend	**pożyczać**
length	**długość**
lens (in glasses)	**szkło**
less	**mniej**
lesson	**lekcja**
to let (allow)	**pozwalać**
to let (rent)	**wynajmować**
letter	**list**
letter (of alphabet)	**litera**
letterbox	**skrzynka pocztowa**
level (height, standard)	**poziom**
level (flat)	**płaski/a/e**
library	**biblioteka**
licence (driving)	**prawo jazdy**
licence (fishing, etc.)	**zezwolenie**
lid	**przykrywka**
life	**życie**
lifebelt	**pas bezpieczeń-stwa**
lifeboat	**łódź ratunkowa**
lifeguard	**ratownik/ ratowniczka**
lifejacket	**kamizelka ratunkowa**
lift (elevator)	**winda**
to lift	**podnosić**
light	**światło**

light (colour)	**jasny/a/e**
light (weight)	**lekki/a/e**
to light (fire, etc.)	**zapalać**
light bulb	**żarówka**
lighter	**zapalniczka**
lightning	**piorun**
like (similar to)	**podobny/a/e**
like this/that	**jak to/tamto**
what is ... like?	**jaki/a/e to jest?**
what are ... like?	**jakie ... są?**
do you like ...?	**czy lubi pan/pani ...?** or **czy podoba się panu/pani ...?**
likely	**prawdopo-dobnie**
limited	**ograniczony/ a/e**
line	**linia**
lion	**lew**
lipstick	**szminka**
liqueur	**likier**
liquid	**płyn**
list	**lista**
to listen	**słuchać**
litre	**litr**
litter (rubbish)	**śmieci**
little (small)	**mały/a/e**
a little	**trochę**
to live	**żyć**
liver	**wątroba**
living room	**pokój stołowy**

loaf (of bread)	**bochenek**	lunch	**obiad**
local	**miejscowy/a/e**		
lock	**zamek**	**M**	
to lock	**zamykać**		
lonely	**samotny/a/e**	mad	**szalony/a/e**
long	**długi/a/e**	madam	**pani**
long johns	**kalesony**	magazine	**pismo**
to look (at)	**patrzeć (na)**	main	**główny/a/e**
to look after	**opiekować się**	make (brand)	**marka**
to look for (sthg)	**szukać**	to make	**robić**
to look like	**wyglądać jak...**	make-up	**makijaż**
loose	**luźny/a/e**	male	**płci męskiej**
lorry	**ciężarówka**	man (male)	**mężczyzna**
lorry driver	**kierowca ciężarówki**	man (human being)	**człowiek**
		manager	**kierownik/ kierowniczka**
to lose	**gubić**		
lost property office	**biuro rzeczy znalezionych**	managing director	**dyrektor/ dyrektorka**
a lot (of)	**dużo**	many	**dużo**
lotion	**płyn**	not many	**nie dużo**
loud	**głośny/a/e**	marble	**marmur**
lounge (hotel)	**hall**	market	**rynek**
love	**miłość**	married (of a man)	**żonaty**
to love	**kochać**	married (of a woman)	**mężatka**
lovely	**śliczny/a/e**	mascara	**tusz do rzęs**
low	**niski/a/e**	masculine	**męski/a/e**
lower	**niższy/a/e**	mass (church)	**msza**
lozenge	**pastylka**	match (sport)	**mecz**
lucky: to be lucky	**mieć szczęście**	to match	**dopasować**
luggage	**bagaż**	matches	**zapałki**
lump (tumour)	**guz**	matter: it doesn't matter	**nie szkodzi**

what's the matter?	o co chodzi?	mild (temperature)	ciepło
mattress	materac	mile	mila
nature	dojrzały/a/e	milk	mleko
me	mi or mnie	milk-shake	koktajl mleczny
meadow	łąka	mill	młynek
meal	posiłek	mince (meat)	mielone (mięso)
mean: what does it mean?	co to znaczy?		
		mind: do you mind ...?	czy pozwoli pan/pani...?
meanwhile	w międzyczasie		
measles	odra	I don't mind	nie mam nic przeciwko
German measles	różyczka		
to measure	mierzyć	mine (of me)	mój/moja/moje
measurement	miara	minister (in politics)	minister
meat	mięso	minute (time)	minuta
cold meats	wędliny	mirror	lustro
medicine (drug)	lekarstwo or lek	Miss	panna
Mediterranean	śródziemno- morski/a/e	to miss (bus etc.)	nie zdążyć na ...
medium (size)	średni/a/e	mist	mgła
meeting	spotkanie	mistake	pomyłka
member	członek	mistaken: to be mistaken	mylić się
to mend	naprawiać	mixed	mieszany/a/e
message	wiadomość	modern	nowoczesny /a/e
meter (in taxi, etc.)	licznik		
microwave (oven)	kuchenka mikrofalowa	moisturizer	nawilżacz
		monastery	klasztor
midday	południe	money	pieniądze
middle	środek	month	miesiąc
middle-aged	w średnim wieku	monument	pomnik
		moon	księżyc
midnight	północ	more	więcej
mild (taste)	łagodny/a/e		

morning	**ranek**
mortgage	**hipoteka**
mosque	**meczet**
mosquito	**komar**
most (of)	**większość**
mother	**matka**
mother-in-law	**teściowa**
motor	**silnik**
motorbike	**motorower**
motorboat	**motorówka**
motor racing	**wyścigi samochodowe**
motorway	**autostrada**
mountain	**góra**
mountaineering	**alpinistyka**
moustache	**wąsy**
mouth	**usta**
to move	**ruszać się**
movement	**ruch**
Mr	**pan**
Mrs	**pani**
much	**dużo**
not much	**nie dużo**
mug	**kubek**
to murder	**mordować**
mushroom	**grzyb**
music	**muzyka**
musician	**muzyk/ muzyczka**
must: it's a must	**koniecznie**
I/you/he/she/it/must	**ja muszę, ty musisz,**

	on/ona/ono musi
my	**mój/moja/moje**

N

nail	**gwóźdź**
nail (finger/toe)	**paznokieć**
nail file	**pilnik do paznokci**
nail polish	**lakier do paznokci**
nail polish remover	**zmywacz do paznokci**
naked	**nagi/a/e**
name	**nazwisko**
first name	**imię**
my name is ...	**nazywam się ...**
what's your name?	**jak się pan/pani nazywa?**
napkin	**serwetka**
nappy	**pieluszka**
narrow	**wąski/a/e**
national	**narodowy/a/e**
nationality	**narodowość**
naughty	**niegrzeczny/a/e**
navy	**marynarka wojenna**
navy-blue	**granatowy/a/e**
near (to)	**blisko**
nearly	**prawie**
necessary	**konieczny/a/e**
necklace	**naszyjnik**

to need	potrzebować
needle	igła
negative (photo)	negatyw
neighbour	sąsiad/ sąsiadka
neither ... nor ...	ani ... ani ...
nephew	siostrzeniec
nervous	nerwowy/a/e
net	siatka
never	nigdy
new	nowy/a/e
New Year	Nowy Rok
news (on TV)	wiadomości
newspaper	gazeta
next	następny/a/e
next week/month/ year	w następnym tygodniu/ miesiącu/roku
nice (person)	miły/a/e
nice (place, etc.)	przyjemny/a/e
niece	siostrzenica
night	noc
nightdress	koszula nocna
no	nie
nobody	nikt
noise	hałas
noisy	hałaśliwy/a/e
non-alcoholic	bezalkoholowy /a/e
non-smoking	niepalący/a/e
normal	normalny/a/e
north	północ

northern	północny/a/e
nose	nos
nosebleed	krew z nosa
not	nie
note (bank)	banknot
notepad	blok
nothing	nic
now	teraz
nowhere	nigdzie
nuclear	nuklearny/a/e
nuclear energy	energia nuklearna
number	numer
nurse	pielęgniarz/ pielęgniarka
nut	orzech
nut (for bolt)	nakrętka

O

oar	wiosło
object	przedmiot
obvious	oczywisty/a/e
occasionally	od czasu do czasu
occupied	zajęty/a/e
odd (peculiar)	dziwny/a/e
odd (not even)	nieparzysty/a/e
of course	oczywiście
off (switched off)	wyłączony/a/e
offended	obrażony/a/e
office (place of work)	biuro

office (secretary's room)	**sekretariat**
office (a room)	**gabinet**
often	**często/a/e**
how often?	**jak często?**
oil	**olej**
OK	**w porządku**
old	**stary/a/e**
how old are you? (formal)	**ile pan/pani ma lat?**
(how old are you? (informal)	**ile masz lat?**
how old is he/she?	**ile on/ona ma lat?**
I'm ... years old	**mam ... lat**
old-fashioned	**staromodny/a/e**
olive	**oliwa**
olive oil	**olej z oliwek**
on	**na**
switched on	**włączony/a/e**
once	**raz**
onion	**cebula**
only	**tylko**
open	**otwarty/a/e**
to open	**otwierać**
opera	**opera**
operation	**operacja**
opinion	**opinia**
in my opinion	**moim zdaniem**
opposite (contrary)	**w przeciwieństwie do**

opposite (on the other side)	**na przeciwko**
optician	**optyk**
or	**albo** or **czy**
orange	**pomarańcza**
orange (colour)	**pomarańczowy /a/e**
order	**zamówienie**
to order	**zamawiać**
ordinary	**zwyczajny/a/e**
to organize	**organizować**
other	**inny/a/e**
others	**inni/** (masculine) **inne** (feminine)
our, ours	**nasz/a/e**
out: he/she is out	**nie ma go/jej**
outdoors	**na wolnym powietrzu**
outside	**na zewnątrz**
over (above)	**nad**
overcoat (short)	**kurtka**
overcoat (long)	**płaszcz**
to overtake	**wyprzedzać**
owner	**właściciel/ właścicielka**

P

package tour holiday	**wczasy zorganizowane**
packet	**paczka**
padlock	**kłódka**
page	**strona**

pain	ból	pastry	ciasto
painful	bolesny/a/e	path	ścieżka
painkiller	środek przeciwbólowy	patient	cierpliwy/a/e
paint	farba	patient (medical)	pacjent/ pacjentka
to paint	malować	pattern	wzór
painter	malarz	pavement	chodnik
painting	obraz	to pay	płacić
pair	para	to pay cash	płacić gotówką
palace	pałac	pea	groszek
pale (of face)	blady/a/e	peace	pokój
pale (colour)	pastelowy/a/e	peach	brzoskwinia
pants (women's underwear)	majtki	peanut	orzeszek ziemny
paper	papier	pear	gruszka
paper clip	spinacz	pedal	pedał
parcel	paczka	pedestrian	pieszy
pardon?	słucham?	pedestrian crossing	przejście dla pieszych
parents	rodzice		
to park	parkować	to peel	obierać
parliament (Polish)	Sejm or parlament	peg	kołek
		pen	pióro
part	część	pencil	ołówek
parting (hair)	przedziałek	pencil sharpener	temperówka
partly	częściowo	penfriend	przyjaciel po piórze
party (celebration)	przyjęcie		
to pass (salt, etc.)	podać	penknife	scyzoryk
to pass (exam)	zdawać	pension (social benefit)	renta
passenger	pasażer/ pasażerka	pension (old age)	emerytura
		pensioner	emeryta/ emerytka
past	przeszłość		
pasta	wyroby z ciasta	people	ludzie

pepper (spice)	**pieprz**	piece	**kawałek**
pepper (plant)	**papryka**	pier	**molo**
peppermint	**mięta**	pig	**świnia**
per	**na**	pill	**pigułka**
perfect	**idealny/a/e**	pill (contraceptive)	**pigułka antykoncepcyjna**
peformance	**przedstawienie**		
performance (cinema)	**seans filmowy**	pillow	**poduszka**
perhaps	**być może**	pillowcase	**poszewka na poduszkę**
period (menstrual)	**period**		
period pains	**ból miesiączkowy**	pin	**szpilka**
		pineapple	**ananas**
perm	**trwała**	pink	**różowy/a/e**
permit	**zezwolenie**	pipe (smoking)	**fajka**
to permit	**zezwalać**	pipe (drain, etc.)	**rura**
person	**osoba**	place	**miejsce**
personal	**osobisty/a/e**	plane (aeroplane)	**samolot**
petrol	**benzyna**	by plane	**samolotem**
petrol can	**puszka z benzyną**	plant	**roślina**
		plaster (on walls, etc.)	**gips**
petrol station	**stacja benzynowa**		
		plastic bag	**torba plastykowa**
petticoat	**koszulka**		
photograph	**zdjęcie**	plate	**talerz**
phrase book	**zbiór wyrażeń i zwrotów**	platform (station)	**peron**
		play (theatre)	**sztuka (teatralna)**
physics	**fizyka**		
piano	**pianino**	to play (instrument)	**grać**
to pick (choose)	**wybierać**	to play (sport)	**uprawiać**
to pick (flowers, etc.)	**zbierać**	pleasant	**przyjemny/a/e**
to pick up	**podnosić**	please	**proszę**
picture	**obraz**	pleased	**zadowolony/a/e**

plenty	dużo
pliers	obcążki
plimsolls	tenisówki
plug (bath)	korek
plug (electrical)	wtyczka
plumber	hydraulik
pneumonia	zapalenie płuc
pocket	kieszeń
point	punkt
poison	trucizna
poisonous	trujący/a/e
pole	biegun
police station	posterunek policji
polish (shoe, etc.)	pasta (do butów)
polite	uprzejmy/a/e
political	polityczny/a/e
politician	polityk
politics	polityka
polluted	zanieczy-szczony /a/e
pollution	zanieczysz-czenie
pool (swimming)	pływalnia or basen kąpielowy
poor	biedny/a/e
Pope	papież
popular	popularny/a/e
pork	wieprzowina
port	port

portable	przenośny/a/e
porter	bagażowy
possible	możliwy/a/e
as ... as possible	tak ... jak to możliwe
if possible	jeżeli to możliwe
possibly	możliwe
post (mail)	poczta
to post	wysyłać pocztą
postbox	skrzynka pocztowa
postcard	karta pocztowa
postcode	kod pocztowy
poster	plakat
postman	listonosz/ listonoszka
post office	poczta
to postpone	przekładać
pot (cooking)	garnek
potato	ziemniak
pottery	garncarstwo
potty (child's)	nocnik
pound (sterling)	funt
to pour	lać
powder	puder
powdery (snow)	sypki/a/e
power	władza
power (electrical)	prąd
power cut	przerwa w dopływie prądu
pram	wózek

to prefer	**woleć**	puncture	**przebita opona**
I prefer	**wolę**	pure	**czysty/a/e**
pregnant	**w ciąży**	purple	**purpurowy/a/e**
to prepare	**przygotowywać**	purse	**portmonetka**
prescription	**recepta**	to push	**pchać**
pretty	**ładny/a/e**	push-chair	**wózek**
price	**cena**	to put	**kłaść**
priest	**ksiądz**	to put down	**odkładać**
prime minister	**premier**	pyjamas	**piżama**
prince	**książę**		
princess	**księżniczka**		
print (photo)	**zdjęcie**	**Q**	
print (picture)	**reprodukcja**	quality	**jakość**
prison	**więzienie**	quarter	**ćwierć**
private	**prywatny/a/e**	quarter (of a town)	**dzielnica**
prize	**nagroda**	quay	**nadbrzeże**
probably	**prawdopod-obnie**	queen	**królowa**
		question	**pytanie**
profession	**zawód**	queue	**kolejka**
profit	**zysk**	quick	**szybki/a/e**
prohibited	**wzbroniony/a/e**	quickly	**szybko**
promise	**obietnica**	quiet	**spokojny/a/e**
to pronounce	**wymawiać**	quite (fairly)	**dosyć**
pronunciation	**wymowa**	quite (completely)	**całkowicie**
properly	**odpowiednio**		
property	**własność**	**R**	
public	**publiczny/a/e**		
public holiday	**dzień wolny od pracy**	rabbit	**królik**
		rabies	**wścieklizna**
to pull	**ciągnąć**	race	**wyścigi**
to pump up	**napompować**	racecourse/track	**tor wyścigowy**
		racing	**wyścigi**

racket (tennis)	**rakieta**
radio station	**radiostacja**
raft	**tratwa**
railway	**kolej**
railway station	**stacja kolejowa**
rain	**deszcz**
to rain	**padać**
it's raining	**pada deszcz**
raincoat	**płaszcz nieprzemakalny**
rainy	**deszczowy/a/e**
to rape	**gwałcić**
rare (infrequent)	**rzadki/a/e**
rare (steak)	**po angielsku**
rash (on skin)	**wysypka**
raspberry	**malina**
rate (speed)	**prędkość**
rate (exchange)	**kurs wymiany**
rather (quite)	**raczej**
raw	**surowy/a/e**
razor	**brzytwa**
to reach/arrive at (on foot)	**przyjść**
to reach/arrive at (by transport)	**przyjechać**
to read	**czytać**
reading	**czytanie**
ready	**gotowy/a/e**
real (authentic)	**prawdziwy/a/e**
really	**rzeczywiście**
rear	**tylny/a/e**
reason	**przyczyna**

the reason why	**przyczyna dla której**
receipt	**pokwitowanie**
to recognize	**poznawać**
to recommend	**polecać**
record (music)	**płyta**
to record	**nagrywać**
red	**czerwony/a/e**
Red Cross	**Czerwony Krzyż**
refill	**nowy zapas**
refill (pen)	**wkład zapasowy**
refrigerator	**lodówka**
to refund	**zwracać pieniądze**
region	**rejon**
to register (oneself)	**zameldować się**
to register (letter)	**wysyłać list polecony**
registration number	**numer rejestracyjny**
relation	**krewny/a**
religion	**religia**
to remain	**zostawać**
to remember	**pamiętać**
I remember	**pamiętam**
to rent	**wynajmować**
rent (money to pay)	**opłata**
to repair	**naprawiać**
to repeat	**powtarzać**

reply	**odpowiedź**
report (business, etc.)	**sprawozdanie**
report (newspaper)	**reportaż**
to report	**zawiadamiać**
to rescue	**ratować**
to reserve	**rezerwować**
reserved (table)	**zarezerwowany /a/e**
responsible	**odpowiedzialny /a/e**
to rest	**odpoczywać**
restaurant car	**wagon restauracyjny**
result	**wynik**
retired	**na rencie**
return	**powrót**
return (ticket)	**powrotny/a/e**
to return (give back)	**zwracać**
to return (oneself)	**wracać**
I return	**wracam**
reversed charge call	**rozmowa na koszt numeru**
rice	**ryż**
rich	**bogaty/a/e**
to ride (a bike/ in a car)	**jechać na rowerze/ samochodem**
to ride a horse	**jeździć konno**
right (direction)	**prawy/a/e**
on/to the right	**na prawo**
right: you are right	**ma pan/pani rację/**
you are not right	**nie ma pan/pani racji**
that's right	**słusznie**
right-hand (side)	**prawa strona**
on the right-hand side	**na prawej stronie**
ring (jewellery)	**pierścionek**
ripe	**dojrzały/a/e**
river	**rzeka**
road	**droga**
to rob	**okradać**
I've been robbed	**okradziono mnie**
robbery	**rozbój**
roof	**dach**
roof-rack	**bagażnik dachowy**
room (house)	**pokój**
room (space)	**przestrzeń**
rope	**lina**
rose	**róża**
rotten	**zgniły/a/e**
rough (surface)	**szorstki/a/e**
rough (sea)	**wzburzony/a/e**
round	**okrągły/a/e**
roundabout (traffic)	**rondo**
roundabout (funfair)	**karuzela**
row (theatre, etc.)	**rząd**
to row	**wiosłować**
rowing boat	**łódź wiosłowa**
royal	**królewski/a/e**
rubber (material)	**guma**

rubber (eraser)	**gumka**
rubber band	**gumka**
rubbish	**śmieci**
rubbish!	**bzdura!**
rucksack	**plecak**
rude	**nieuprzejmy/a/e**
ruins	**ruiny**
ruler (measuring)	**linijka**
to run	**biegać**
rush-hour	**godzina szczytu**
rusty	**zardzewiały/a/e**

S

sad	**smutny/a/e**
safe (strongbox)	**sejf**
safe	**bezpieczny/a/e**
safety pin	**agrafka**
sail	**żagiel**
sailing	**żeglarstwo**
sailing boat	**żaglówka**
sailor	**marynarz**
saint	**święty/a/e**
sale	**sprzedaż**
salesman	**sprzedawca**
saleswoman	**sprzedawczyni**
sales representative	**przedstawiciel do spraw handlowych**
salmon	**łosoś**
salt	**sól**

salty	**słony/a/e**
same	**ten sam/ta sama/to samo**
sample	**próbka**
sand	**piasek**
sandwich	**kanapka**
sanitary towel	**opaska higieniczna**
sauce	**sos**
saucepan	**garnek**
saucer	**spodek**
to save (rescue)	**ratować**
to save (money)	**oszczędzać**
to say	**mówić**
how do you say it?	**jak to się mówi?**
people say that ...	**ludzie mówią że ...**
that is to say ...	**to znaczy ...**
scales (weighing)	**waga**
scarf	**szalik**
scene (theatre)	**scena**
scene (view)	**widok**
scenery (countryside)	**krajobraz**
scent	**zapach**
school	**szkoła**
science	**nauka ścisła**
scientist	**naukowiec**
scissors	**nożyczki**
score: what's the score?	**jaki wynik?**

final score	**wynik końcowy**	self-catering	**bez wyżywienia**
scratch	**rysa**	self-service	**samoobsługa**
scratch (on skin)	**zadrapanie**	to sell	**sprzedawać**
screen (cinema, etc.)	**ekran**	to send	**wysyłać**
screen (partition)	**parawan**	senior citizen	**emeryt/**
screw	**śrubka**		**emerytka**
screwdriver	**śrubokręt**	sensible	**rozsądny/a/e**
sculpture	**rzeźba**	sentence	**zdanie**
sea	**morze**	sentence (prison)	**wyrok**
seasick	**cierpiący na**	separate, separated	**osobny/a/e**
	chorobę	serious	**poważny/a/e**
	morską	serious (important)	**ważny/a/e**
season (of year)	**sezon**	to serve	**służyć**
season ticket	**bilet sezonowy**	service (church)	**msza**
seat (place on the train, etc.)	**miejsce**	service charge	**opłata za**
			obsługę
seat (chair)	**krzesło**	set (group)	**zestaw**
seat-belt	**pas**	set (series)	**seria**
	bezpieczeń-	setting lotion	**płyn**
	stwa		**utrwalający**
second	**drugi/a/e**	several	**kilka**
second (time)	**sekunda**	to sew	**szyć**
second-hand	**używany/a/e**	sewing	**szycie**
secret	**tajemnica**	sex (gender)	**płeć**
secret	**tajny/a/e**	sex (intercourse)	**stosunek**
secretary	**sekretarz/**		**płciowy**
	sekretarka	shade (colour)	**odcień**
section	**sekcja**	shadow	**cień**
to see	**widzieć**	shampoo	**szampon**
I (can't) see it	**(nie) widzę**	shampoo and blow-dry	**uczesanie z**
to seem	**wydawać się**		**umyciem głowy**
it seems ...	**wydaje się**	sharp	**ostry/a/e**

o shave	golić	shower	prysznic
having cream	krem do golenia	to shrink	kurczyć się
he	ona	shut	zamknięty/a/e
heep	owca	shutter (window)	żaluzja
heet	prześcieradło	shutter (camera)	przesłona
helf	półka	sick (ill)	chory/a/e
hell (egg)	skorupka	to be sick	wymiotować
hell (sea)	muszelka	to feel sick	mieć nudności
hellfish	skorupiaki	side	strona
helter	schronienie	sieve	sito
hiny	błyszczący/a/e	sight (vision)	wzrok
hip	statek	sights (tourist)	widoki
hirt	koszula	sightseeing	zwiedzanie
hock	szok	sign	znak
hoe	but	to sign (one's name)	podpisać
hoelace	sznurowadło	signature	podpis
hoe polish	pasta do butów	silent	cichy/a/e
hoe shop	sklep z obuwiem	silk	jedwab
		silver	srebro
hop	sklep	similar (to)	podobny (do)
hop assistant	sprzedawca/ sprzedawczyni	simple	prosty/a/e
		since	od
		to sing	śpiewać
hopping: to go hopping	iść na zakupy	single (room)	na jedną osobę
		single (ticket)	w jedną stronę
hopping centre	centrum handlowe	single (unmarried)	samotny/a/e
hort	krótki/a/e	single (record)	single
horts	szorty	sink	zlew
o shout	krzyczeć	sir	pan
how	pokaz	sister	siostra
o show	pokazywać	sister-in-law	szwagierka

to sit (down)	**siadać**
sit down (polite)	**proszę usiąść**
size (dimension)	**rozmiar**
size (shoes)	**numer**
skates (on ice)	**łyżwy**
to skate	**jeździć na łyżwach**
skis	**narty**
to ski	**jeździć na nartach**
ski boot	**but narciarski**
skiing	**jazda na nartach**
ski lift	**wyciąg narciarski**
skimmed milk	**mleko odtłuszczone**
skin	**skóra**
skin-diving	**nurkowanie**
ski pole	**kijek narciarski**
skirt	**spódnica**
ski run	**stok narciarski**
ski suit	**strój narciarski**
sky	**niebo**
to sleep	**spać**
sleeper (on train)	**wagon sypialny**
sleeve	**rękaw**
slice	**kawałek**
sliced	**pokrojony/a/e**
slide (film)	**przeźrocze**
slim	**szczupły/a/e**
slip (petticoat)	**koszulka**

slippery	**śliski/a/e**
slow	**powolna/e**
slowly	**powoli**
small	**mały/a/e**
smell	**zapach**
smell: it smells bad	**śmierdzi**
it smells good	**ładnie pachnie**
smile	**uśmiech**
smoke	**dym**
to smoke	**palić**
smoked	**wędzony/a/e**
smooth	**gładki/a/e**
snake	**wąż**
to sneeze	**kichać**
snow	**śnieg**
snow: it's snowing	**pada śnieg**
so (thus)	**więc**
soap	**mydło**
sober	**trzeźwy/a/e**
social worker	**pracownik socjalny**
sock	**skarpetka**
socket (electrical)	**gniazdko**
soda (water)	**sodowa (woda)**
soft	**miękki/a/e**
soft drinks	**napoje bezalkoholowe**
soldier	**żołnierz**
sold out	**wyprzedane**
so many/so much	**tak dużo**
some	**trochę**

somehow	jakoś	special	specjalny/a/e
someone	ktoś	specialty	specjalność
something	coś	spectacles	okulary
sometimes	czasami	speed	prędkość
somewhere	gdzieś	speed limit	ograniczenie prędkości
son	syn		
song	piosenka	to spend (money)	wydawać
son-in-law	zięć	to spend (time)	spędzać
soon	wkrótce	spice	przyprawa
as soon as possible	jak najszybciej	spicy	pikantny/a/e
sore throat	ból gardła	spinach	szpinak
sorry (pardon me)	przepraszam	spirits (alcohol)	alkohole
I'm sorry	przepraszam	splinter	drzazga
sort (type)	rodzaj	to spoil	psuć
sound	dźwięk	sponge	gąbka
soup	zupa	sponge (cake)	biszkopt
sour	kwaśny/a/e	spoon	łyżka
south	południe	spot	punkt
southern	południowy/a/e	sprain	zwichnięcie
souvenir	upominek	sprained	zwichnięty/a/e
space	przestrzeń	spray	rozpylacz
spade	łopata	spring (season)	wiosna
spanner	klucz do nakrętek	square (town)	plac
		square (shape)	kwadrat
spare (available)	zapasowy/a/e	stadium	stadion
spare (left over)	resztki	stain	plama
spare time	wolny czas	stainless steel	stal nierdzewna
spare wheel	koło zapasowe	stairs	schody
sparkling (wine)	(wino) musujące	stalls (theatre)	parter
		stamp (postage)	znaczek
to speak	mówić	stand (podium)	trybuna

standing (up)	**stojąc**	to stick	**naklejać**
stapler	**spinacz**	sticking plaster	**plaster**
star	**gwiazda**	sticky	**lepki/a/e**
start (beginning)	**początek**	stiff	**sztywny/a/e**
to start	**zaczynać**	still	**spokojny/a/e**
starter (food)	**zakąska**	still (non-fizzy)	**nie**
state	**państwo**		**gazowany/a/e**
station	**stacja**	sting	**żądło**
station master	**zawiadowca**	to sting (insect)	**żądlić**
	stacji	stock exchange	**giełda**
stationer's	**papeteria**	stockings	**pończochy**
statue	**posąg**	stolen: my ... has	**ukradziono**
stay	**pobyt**	been stolen	**mi ...**
stay: I'm staying at ...	**mieszkam w ...**	stomach	**żołądek**
steak	**befsztyk**	stomach-ache	**ból żołądka**
to steal	**kraść**	stomach upset	**niestrawność**
steam	**para**	stone	**kamień**
steel	**stal**	stop (bus)	**przystanek**
steep	**stromy/a/e**	to stop	**zatrzymywać**
step (walking)	**krok**		**się**
step (stair)	**stopień**	stop!	**stop!**
stepbrother	**brat przyrodni**	stopcock	**kurek**
stepchildren	**pasierbowie**		**zamykający**
stepdaughter	**pasierbica**	storey	**piętro**
stepfather	**ojczym**	story	**historia**
stepmother	**macocha**	stove	**piec**
stepsister	**siostra**	straight	**prosty/a/e**
	przyrodnia	straight on	**prosto**
stepson	**pasierb**	strange	**dziwny/a/e**
sterling: pound sterling	**funt**	strap	**rzemień**
	angielski	straw (drinking)	**słomka**
stick	**kij**	strawberry	**truskawka**

stream	strumień
street	ulica
street light	lampa uliczna
stretcher	nosze
strike (work)	strajk
string	sznurek
stripe	pasek
striped	w paski
strong	silny/a/e
to study	studiować
stupid	głupi/a/e
style	styl
styling mousse	mus do układania włosów
subtitled	z napisami
suburbs	peryferie
to succeed/be successful	odnosić sukces
success	sukces
such	taki/a/e
suddenly	nagle
sugar	cukier
sugar lump	kostka cukru
suit (clothes)	garnitur
suitcase	walizka
summer	lato
sun	słońce
to sunbathe	opalać się
sunburn	oparzenie słońcem
sunglasses	okulary słoneczne
sunshade	parasol
sunstroke	udar słoneczny
suntan cream	krem do opalania
supermarket	Sam
supper	kolacja
supplement	dodatek
suppose: I suppose so/not	chyba tak/nie
suppository	czopek
sure	pewny/a/e
surface	powierzchnia
surname	nazwisko
surprise	niespodzianka
surprised	zdziwiony/a/e
surrounded (by)	otoczony/a/e (przez)
to sweat	pocić się
sweater	sweter
sweatshirt	bluza sportowa
to sweep	zamiatać
sweet	słodki/a/e
sweetener	słodzik
sweets	słodycze
swelling	opuchlina
to swim	pływać
swimming	pływanie
swimming pool	pływalnia or basen kąpielowy

swimming trunks	spodenki kąpielowe	tape measure	centymetr (krawiecki)
switch	kontakt	tape recorder	magnetofon
to switch off (light)	wyłączać	taste	smak
to switch off (engine)	zgasić	tasty	smaczny/a/e
to switch on	włączać	tax	podatek
how do you switch it on?	jak to się włącza?	taxi rank	postój taksówek
swollen	spuchnięty/a/e	tea	herbata
		tea bag	herbata z torebki

T

table	stół	to teach	uczyć
tablet	tabletka	teacher	nauczyciel/ nauczycielka
table tennis	ping-pong	team	drużyna
tailor	krawiec	teapot	czajniczek
to take	brać,	to tear	drzeć
to take (bus, etc.)	jechać (autobusem itd.)	teaspoon	łyżeczka
		teat (for baby's bottle)	smoczek
to take time	nie spieszyć się	tea-towel	ścierka
to take out	wyjmować	technical	techniczny/a/e
taken (seat)	zajęty/a/e	teenager	nastolatek/ nastolatka
to take off (plane)	startować		
to take (remove)	zdejmować	telephone directory	książka telefoniczna
talcum powder	talk		
to talk	rozmawiać	to telephone	dzwonić
tall	wysoki/a/e	television	telewizja
tame	oswojony/a/e	to tell	mówić
tap	kurek	temperature	gorączka
tape	taśma	to have a temperature	mieć gorączkę

temporary	tymczasowy/a/e	thin (people)	chudy/a/e
		thing	rzecz
tender (meat)	miękki/a/e	to think	myśleć
tennis	tenis	I think so/not	myślę że tak/myślę że nie
tennis courts	korty tenisowe		
tennis shoes/trainers	adidasy	third	trzeci/a/e
tent	namiot	thirsty: I'm thirsty	chce mi się pić
tent peg	śledź	this (one)	ten/ta/to
terrace	taras	those	tamci (male), tamte (female)
terrible	okropny/a/e		
thank you (very much)	dziękuję (bardzo)	thread	nitka
		throat	gardło
that (that one)	tamten/tamta/tamto	throat lozenges/pastilles	pastylki do ssania
theatre	teatr	through	przez
their/theirs	ich	to throw	rzucać
them	im/nimi/nich/nie (case)	to throw away	wyrzucać
		thumb	kciuk
then (at that time)	wtedy	thunder	grzmot
then (later on)	później	ticket	bilet
there	tam	ticket office	kasa
therefore	dlatego	tide: high/low	przypływ/odpływ
there is/are	jest/są		
thief	złodziej/złodziejka	tidy	porządny/a/e
		tie	krawat
these	ci (male), te (female)	tight	ciasny/a/e
		tights	rajstopy
they	oni (male), one (female)	till (until)	do
		time (once, etc.)	czas
thick (fat)	gruby/a/e	time	godzina
thick (slow)	powolny/a/e	there is no time	nie ma czasu
thin (things)	cienki/a/e		

timetable	plan or rozkład jazdy	tonight	dziś wieczorem
		too (also)	też
tin	puszka	too (excessively)	za
tinfoil	folia cynowa	too many/much	za dużo
tinned	puszkowany/a/e	tool	narzędzie
		tooth	ząb
tin-opener	otwieracz do puszek	toothache	ból zęba
		toothbrush	szczoteczka do zębów
tip (money)	napiwek		
tired	zmęczony/a/e	toothpaste	pasta do zębów
tissues	chusteczki z papieru	toothpick	wykałaczka
		top (of mountain)	szczyt
to	do	on top (of)	na górze
toast (cheers)	toast	top floor	górne piętro
toast (bread)	grzanka	torch	latarka
tobacco	tytoń	torn	podarty/a/e
tobacconist's	sklep z wyrobami tytoniowymi	total (money)	suma ogólna
		total (complete)	całkowity/a/e
today	dzisiaj or dziś	to touch	dotykać
together	razem	tough (meat)	twardy/a/e
toilet	ubikacja or toaleta	tour (excursion)	wycieczka
		tourism	turystyka
toilet- paper	papier toaletowy	tourist	turysta
		tourist information office	biuro informacji turystycznej
toiletries	artykuły kosmetyczne		
toilet water	woda toaletowa	to tow	holować
toll	opłata rogatkowa	towards	w kierunku
		towel	ręcznik
tomato	pomidor	tower	wieża
tomorrow	jutro	town	miasto
tongue	język	town centre	centrum

town hall	ratusz	trout	pstrąg
towrope	lina holownicza	true	prawdziwy/a/e
toy	zabawka	to try	próbować
track (path)	ścieżka	to try on	przymierzać
tracksuit	dresy	T-shirt	koszulka
trade union	związek zawodowy	tuna	tuńczyk
traffic	ruch drogowy	tunnel	tunel
traffic jam	korek drogowy	to turn	kręcić
traffic lights	światła ruchu drogowego	turning (side road)	zakręt
		to turn off	skręcać
trailer	przyczepa	to turn off (engine)	gasić
train	pociąg	to turn off (tap)	wyłączyć
by train	pociągiem	to turn on	włączyć
training shoes	trampki or adidasy	twice	dwa razy
		twins	bliźniaki
tram	tramwaj	twisted	kręcony/a/e
tranquillizer	środek uspokajający	type (sort)	rodzaj
		to type	pisać na maszynie
to translate	tłumaczyć		
translation	tłumaczenie	typewriter	maszyna do pisania
to travel	podróżować		
travel agency	biuro podróży	typical	typowy/a/e
traveller's cheque	czek podróżny		
travel-sickness	choroba morska	**U**	
tray	taca	ugly	brzydki/a/e
treatment	leczenie	ulcer	wrzód
tree	drzewo	umbrella	parasolka
trip	wycieczka	uncle	wujek
trolley	wózek	uncomfortable	niewygodny/a/e
trousers	spodnie	under	pod
		underground	podziemie

183

underneath	**pod spodem**
underpants	**majtki**
to understand	**rozumieć**
underwater	**pod wodą**
unemployed	**bezrobotny/a/e**
unfortunately	**niestety**
unhappy	**nieszczęśliwy /a/e** or **smutny/ a/e**
uniform	**mundur**
unless	**jeżeli nie**
unpleasant	**nieprzyjemny /a/e**
to unscrew	**odkręcać**
until	**aż do**
unusual	**niezwykły/a/e**
unwell	**niedobrze**
up	**w górę**
upper	**górny/a/e**
upstairs	**na górze**
urgent	**pilny/a/e**
urine	**mocz**
us	**nas/nami** (case)
use	**użycie**
to use	**używać**
useful	**pożyteczny/a/e**
useless	**bezużyteczny /a/e**
usual: as usual	**jak zwykle**
usually	**zwykle**

V

vacant	**wolny/a/e**
vacuum cleaner	**odkurzacz**
vacuum flask	**termos**
valid	**ważny/a/e**
valley	**dolina**
valuable	**cenny/a/e**
valuables	**cenne rzeczy**
van	**furgonetka**
vanilla	**wanilia**
vase	**wazon**
VAT	**VAT**
veal	**cielęcina**
vegetable	**jarzyna**
vegetarian	**jarosz**
vehicle	**pojazd**
vermouth	**wermut**
very/very much	**bardzo**
vest	**koszulka**
vet	**weterynarz**
via	**przez**
video cassette	**kaseta magnetowidu**
video recorder	**magnetowid**
view	**widok**
villa	**willa**
village	**wieś**
vinegar	**ocet**
vineyard	**winnica**
virgin	**dziewica**

Virgin Mary	**Maria Panna**	washable	**nadający/a/e się do prania**
visit	**wizyta**		
to visit (places)	**zwiedzać**	washbasin	**umywalka**
to visit (people)	**odwiedzać**	washing	**pranie**
visitor	**zwiedzający/a/e**	washing powder	**proszek do prania**
voice	**głos**		
volleyball	**siatkówka**	to wash up	**pozmywać**
voltage	**napięcie**	washing-up liquid	**płyn do zmywania**
to vote	**głosować**		
		wasp	**osa**

W

		wastepaper basket	**kosz na papiery**
wage	**zapłata**	watch (wristwatch)	**zegarek**
waist	**talia**	to watch (TV, etc.)	**oglądać**
waistcoat	**kamizelka**	watchstrap	**pasek do zegarka**
to wait (for)	**czekać (na)**		
waiter, waitress	**kelner, kelnerka**	water	**woda**
		waterfall	**wodospad**
waiting-room	**poczekalnia**	waterproof	**nieprzemakalny /a/e**
walk	**spacer**		
to go for a walk	**iść na spacer**	water-skiing	**narty wodne**
to walk	**spacerować**	wave (sea)	**fala**
walking stick	**laska**	wax	**wosk**
wall (house)	**ściana**	way (route)	**droga**
wall (outside)	**mur**	that way	**w tamtę stronę**
wallet	**portfel**	this way	**w tę stronę**
walnut	**orzech włoski**	way (method)	**sposób**
to want	**chcieć**	way in	**wejście**
war	**wojna**	way out	**wyjście**
warm	**ciepły/a/e**	we	**my**
to wash	**prać**	weather	**pogoda**
		what's the weather like?	**jaka jest pogoda?**

wedding	**ślub**	whole	**cały/a/e**
week	**tydzień**	wholemeal bread	**chleb razowy**
weekday	**dzień tygodnia**	whose	**czyj/a/e**
weekend	**koniec tygodnia**	why?	**dlaczego?**
		why not?	**dlaczego nie?**
weekly	**tygodniowy/a/e**	wide	**szeroki/a/e**
to weigh	**ważyć**	widow	**wdowa**
weight	**waga**	widower	**wdowiec**
welcome	**witaj** (singular) **witajcie** (plural)	wife	**żona**
		wild	**dziki/a/e**
well (water)	**studnia**	win	**wygrana**
well (adverb)	**dobrze**	to win	**wygrywać**
well done (steak)	**dobrze wysmażony/a/e**	who won?	**kto wygrał?**
		wind	**wiatr**
west	**zachodni/a/e**	windmill	**wiatrak**
wet	**mokry/a/e**	window	**okno**
wet suit	**kombinezon do nurkowania**	window shop	**wystawa**
		windy: it's windy	**wieje wiatr**
what	**co**	wing	**skrzydło**
what is it?	**co to jest?**	winter	**zima**
wheel	**koło**	with	**z** or **ze**
wheelchair	**wózek inwalidzki**	without	**bez, beze**
when	**kiedy**	woman	**kobieta**
where	**gdzie**	wonderful	**cudowny/a/e**
where is/are ...?	**gdzie jest/są ...?**	wood (trees)	**las**
which	**który/a/e**	wood (material)	**drewno**
while (moment)	**chwila**	wool	**wełna**
while (during)	**podczas**	word	**słowo**
white	**biały/a/e**	work	**praca**
who	**kto**	to work	**pracować**
who is it?	**kto to jest?**	world	**świat**

world (of the world)	światowy/a/e
First/Second World War	pierwsza/ druga wojna światowa
worried	zmartwiony/a/e
to worry	martwić się
don't worry	nie martw się
worse	gorszy/a/e
worth: it's worth ...	jest warty/a/e ...
it's not worth ...	nie jest warty/a/e ...
would like: I would like	chciałbym (male)/ chciałabym (female)
wound (injury)	rana
to wrap (up)	zawijać
to write	pisać
writer	pisarz/pisarka
writing paper	papier do pisania
wrong	niewłaściwy/a/e
you're wrong	nie ma pan/ pani racji
there's something wrong	coś jest niedobrze

X

X-ray	prześwietlenie

Y

yacht	jacht
to yawn	ziewać
year	rok
yellow	żółty/a/e
yes	tak
yesterday	wczoraj
yet	jeszcze
not yet	jeszcze nie
you (informal singular)	ty
you (informal plural)	wy
you (formal singular)	pan/pani
you (formal plural)	państwo
young	młody/a/e
your (informal singular)	twój/twoja/ twoje
your (informal plural)	wasz/wasza/ wasze
your (formal singular)	pana/pani
your (formal plural)	państwa
youth	młodość
youth hostel	schronisko młodzieżowe

Z

zip	zamek błyskawiczny
zoo	zoo
zoology	zoologia

Emergencies

(see also Problems and complaints, page 97)

You may want to say

Phoning the emergencies services

(I need) the police, please	**Policja**	*poleetsya*
(I need) the fire brigade, please	**Straż pożarna**	*strash pozharna*
(I need) an ambulance, please	**Pogotowie**	*pogotovye*
It's my husband/son	**To mój mąż/syn**	*to mooy monsh/sin*
It's my wife/daughter	**To moja żona/córka**	*to moya zhona /tsoorka*
Please come immediately	**Proszę natychmiast przyjść/przyjechać**	*prosheh natihmyast pshiyshch/ pshiyehach*
Where is the police station?	**Gdzie jest posterunek policji?**	*gdje yest posteroonek poleetsee*
Where is the hospital?	**Gdzie jest szpital?**	*gdje yest shpeetal*

You may hear

When you phone the emergency services

Co się stało?	*tso sheh stawo*	What happened?
Nazwisko i adres proszę	*nazveesko ee adres prosheh*	Your name and address please

Wysyłamy kogoś z policji	visiwami kogosh s poleetsii	We're sending someone from the police station
Zaraz przyjedzie straż pożarna	zaras pshiyedje strash pozharna	A fire engine is on the way
Zaraz przyjedzie pogotowie	zaras pshiyedje pogotovye	An ambulance is on the way

'Emergency' exclamations

Help!	Pomocy!	pomotsi
Police!	Policja!	poleetsya
Get out of the way	Z drogi!	z drogee
Call the fire brigade	Zadzwonić po straż pożarną	zadzvoneech po strash pozharno
Call an ambulance	Zadzwonić po pogotowie	zadzvoneech po pogotovye
Stop thief!	Zatrzymać złodzieja!	zatshimach zwodjeya
Look out!	Uważaj!	oovazhay
Fire!	Pożar!	pozhar
Get a doctor	Zawołać doktora	zavowach doktora
Get help quickly	Pomocy, szybko	pomotsi shipko
It's an emergency	To nagły wypadek	to nagwi vipadek

Emergency telephone numbers

997	Police
998	Fire brigade
999	Ambulance
901	International operator

I want the number for ...	Chcę numer...	htseh noomer
Police	Policja	poleetsya
Fire brigade	Straż pożarna	strash pozharna
Ambulance	Pogotowie	pogotovye

All-purpose phrases

Hallo (informal)	**Cześć**	*cheshch*
Good morning	**Dzień dobry**	*djen dobry*
Good evening	**Dobry wieczór**	*dobri vyechoor*
Good night	**Dobranoc**	*dobranots*
Goodbye	**Do widzenia**	*do veedzenya*
Yes	**Tak**	*tak*
No	**Nie**	*nye*
Please	**Proszę**	*prosheh*
Thank you (very much)	**Dziękuję (bardzo)**	*djenkooyeh (bardzo)*
Don't mention it	**Nie ma za co**	*nye ma za tso*
I don't know	**Nie wiem**	*nye vyem*
I don't understand	**Nie rozumiem**	*nye rozoomyem*
I speak very little Polish	**Mówię bardzo mało po polsku**	*moovyeh bardzo mawo po polskoo*
Pardon?	**Słucham?**	*swooham*
Can you repeat that?	**Proszę powtórzyć**	*prosheh poftoozhich*
More slowly, please	**Powoli, proszę**	*povolee prosheh*
Again, please	**Jeszcze raz, proszę**	*yeshche ras, prosheh*
Can you show me in the book?	**Proszę pokazać w książce**	*prosheh pokazach f kshonshtse*
Can you write it down?	**Czy może pan/pani to napisać?**	*chi mozhe pan/panee to napeesach*
Do you speak English?	**Czy mówi pan/pani po angielsku?**	*chi moovee pan/panee po angyelskoo*
Is there anyone who speaks English?	**Czy mówi ktoś po angielsku?**	*chi moovee ktosh po angyelskoo*
Can you help me?	**Czy może mi pan/pani pomóc?**	*chi mozhe mee pan/panee pomoots*

What is this?	**Co to jest?**	*tso to yest*
What is it called in Polish?	**Jak to się nazywa po polsku?**	*yak to sheh naziva po polskoo*
Excuse me/Sorry	**Przepraszam**	*psheprasham*
I'm sorry	**Przepraszam**	*psheprasham*
OK, fine/Very well	**Dobrze/Bardzo dobrze**	*dobzhe/bardzo dobzhe*
That's all right	**W porządku**	*f pozhontkoo*
That's true/right	**To prawda**	*to pravda*
Really/Is that so?	**Naprawdę?**	*napravdeh*
It doesn't matter	**Nie szkodzi**	*nye shkodjee*
Is/Are there (any) ...?	**Czy jest/Czy są (jakieś) ...?**	*chi yest/chi so (yakyesh)*
Is there any milk?	**Czy jest mleko?**	*chi yest mleko*
Are there any tomatoes?	**Czy są pomidory?**	*chi so pomeedori*
Do you have ...?	**Czy ma pan/pani ...?**	*chi ma pan/panee*
Where is/are ...?	**Gdzie jest/są ...?**	*gdje yest/so*
Where are the toilets?	**Gdzie jest ubikacja?**	*gdje yest oobeekatsya*
Where are the taxis?	**Gdzie są taksówki?**	*gdje so taxoofkee*
What time is it?	**Która godzina?**	*ktoora godjeena*
How much is it?	**Ile to kosztuje?**	*eele to koshtooye*
Can I/we ...?/Is it possible to ...?	**Czy można ...?**	*chi mozhna*
Can I/we park here?	**Czy można tu zaparkować?**	*chi mozhna too zaparkovach*
What is the matter?	**Co się dzieje?**	*tso sheh djeye*

BBC Books publishes courses on the following languages:

ARABIC	ITALIAN
CHINESE	JAPANESE
FRENCH	PORTUGUESE
GERMAN	RUSSIAN
GREEK	SPANISH
HINDI & URDU	TURKISH

Developed by BBC Language Unit
Cover designed by Peter Bridgewater and Annie Moss
Project Manager: Stenton Associates
Design: Steve Pitcher
Series Editor: Carol Stanley

Published by BBC Books
A division of BBC Worldwide Ltd
Woodlands, 80 Wood Lane, London W12 OTT

ISBN 0563 39904 X

First published 1995

Text and Cover printed in Great Britain by Clays Ltd,
St Ives Plc